Disclaimer

The information included in this book is designed to provide helpful information on the subjects discussed. This book is not meant to be used to diagnose or treat any medical condition. For diagnosis or treatment of any medical problem, consult your own doctor. The author and publisher are not responsible for any specific health or allergy needs that may require medical supervision and are not liable for any damages or negative consequences from any application, action, treatment, or preparation, to anyone reading or following the information in this book. Links may change and any references included are provided for informational purposes only.

Business Plan

The Right Way To Create A Winning Business Plan

By Susan Hollister

Table of Contents

INTRODUCTION 4

CHAPTER 1: THE BASICS OF BUSINESS PLANNING 8

CHAPTER 2: COMMON MISTAKES PEOPLE MAKE AND HOW TO AVOID THEM 22

CHAPTER 3: BEGINNING THE PLANNING PROCESS 31

CHAPTER 4: WRITING YOUR EXECUTIVE SUMMARY.................37

CHAPTER 5: YOUR COMPANY DESCRIPTION AND MISSION STATEMENT..42

CHAPTER 6: DESCRIBING YOUR PRODUCT OR SERVICE.............58

CHAPTER 7: INDUSTRY AND MARKET ANALYSIS.......................63

CHAPTER 8: DEFINING YOUR COMPANY'S OPERATIONS 74

CHAPTER 9: BUILDING AND DESCRIBING YOUR MANAGEMENT TEAM 82

CHAPTER 10: ANALYZE YOUR COMPETITION...........................88

CHAPTER 11: DEVELOPING YOUR MARKETING STRATEGY.........93

CHAPTER 12: REVENUE, EXPENSES, AND FINANCIAL PLANNING 101

CHAPTER 13: FUNDING STRATEGIES 105

CONCLUSION 111

MY OTHER BOOKS 112

Introduction

So you've finally gathered up enough courage to start your very own business! Congratulations – many aspiring business owners don't even make it past their vision. Starting your own business is often part of the big "Dream"...what could be better than being your own boss? You can take off whenever you want, have more control over your life and you can delegate work for other people to help you. The only person you'll need to answer to is yourself and you'll be at the top of the food chain!

Your product or service will be so ingenious that it will naturally catch on, and become a trending item that will make you millions! You'll be able to sit back and reap the benefits of your positions as "CEO," "President," "Owner," etc. Life will be grand! Once you've got your business products and/or services in place, you'll never need to lift a finger again!

BUT WAIT!

While most of those ideas easily ring true, given the perfect amount of smart strategies, dedication, and commitment, along with the right idea, there is one key aspect that holds it all together and can dramatically transform your dream into a reality: **planning.** Though it is tempting to think that once you create a product or design a service and put it out there for the world to utilize, you'll become instantly rich or famous, there are a few details you simply must work out before you can sit back and watch your business grow.

Starting a business is fairly easy; just about anyone can do it. All you have to do is to file a few papers within your state government and other entities. It's fairly simple to start out as small proprietorship or LLC; from that place, you can quickly grow into a large corporation and a winning concern... but what determines whether a new business booms or it crashes and burns right before the owner's very eyes?

According to the Small Business Association (SBA), entrepreneurs fire up an average of 543,000 small businesses every MONTH...but only 25% of those businesses will survive to reach the 15-year mark. While 70% will make it past the first two years, 50% will have dissolved by the fifth year and only 30% make it to ten years.

Why?

While there are many factors that can influence whether a business sinks or floats, a big one rests on the **business plan.** A business plan is an official written document that defines the business's goals, determines whether those goals are attainable, and then lays out a specific plan for achieving them. A typical business plan includes information on the company, the products or services it offers, its market, a marketing strategy, and a financial plan.

A business plan is a living document, not something you write and then forget about. Business plans help companies track and manage market changes, adjust to shifting trends and financial winds, and it is commonly used to find funding and investors, all of which can play a huge part in determining whether the business will be left on its last leg. It can be used to keep a product or service ahead of the game so that the market demand never dies out and that the company stays ahead of its competition. A business plan is what keeps a company together and what helps its employees make the best decisions possible. Most often, business plans are created prior to the creation of a start-up or in its very early stages and is then revisited at different points throughout the company's lifespan.

As a business owner, you can indeed do whatever you want. A business plan is not required to create or own a business. However, it is strongly recommended, if you want your business to grow and become successful. I have a true story to drive this point home:

Denise, a close friend of mine, "accidentally" created her own business when she discovered that she could make money by writing website content for business owners who lacked the time or skill to do this for themselves. Denise soon realized success as a freelance writer and began to advertise her services in the hopes of making more money. What started out as writing a couple of articles for a few clients quickly spiraled into an overwhelming demand for more than just website content – she was getting requests for resumes, promotional articles, press releases, brochures and pamphlets, editing services, fiction pieces, and even full-blown books to be published by clients all over the world!

While Denise was undoubtedly a talented writer, she soon began to realize that she was only one person and could only take on so many writing jobs at a time. Taking on too much without a plan and the necessary knowledge in place led to some pretty rough pitfalls – once she spent months writing a book for a client overseas who promised her a $75 payment. When she received the payment, it turned out to be in Shekels, not American Dollars, which amounted to about $3 in American currency. Denise couldn't do anything about it because she had dived into the job head-on without the slightest mention of a contract. The process of selecting clients based on her availability always left her with a pit in her stomach; it meant she was losing potential money and networking opportunities.

Luckily, Denise was smart enough to realize that she needed to work on formalizing her business, which included developing a business plan to help her spell out the details of what she needed to do to become a successful business owner and keep her work manageable. She easily caught on to the process of creating a business plan and this helped her define the types of writing services she would offer and to whom, how she would market her services, and how she would organize and track her finances. Her business plan enabled her to define and prioritize her own business goals, such as learning important ethical business practices that included always working from a contract, in order to protect herself and her hard work.

Denise reviewed her business plan once every quarter to determine if she needed to change or update her business goals, make any adjustments to her financial plan based on her revenue, adjust her target audience or marketing plan, or shift her focus to keep aligned with her stated purpose. As a result, she was able to determine which clients had the best chances of becoming repeat customers, which clients were worth working with, which social media channels were most efficient in advertising her services, and determine in which direction her business was headed.

The business plan helped Denise improve the stability and success of her business, so much so that after a few years, she was confident and ready to explore plans to expand her business. By taking on a few employees, she would be able to double the writing work she could do — thereby opening up the possibility of doubling her revenue and possibly moving her business one step closer to corporation status.

Had Denise neglected to create a business plan, it's likely that she would have grown frustrated and overwhelmed with the work; she could have easily thrown in the towel well before the two year mark. Today, Denise's business is going on five years of strong financial growth. She's already past the 50% success mark and it looks like she'll make it to the top 30%. She credits most of her success to having a plan.

This book contains step-by-step guidance and proven strategies that can help you write a solid business plan that will increase the chances of YOUR business being successful and reaching the 15 year mark and more!

Chapter 1: The Basics of Business Planning

In the introduction, you discovered some ways in which a business plan can have a huge impact on your success. In addition to the key points I highlighted in Denise's story, here are some reasons why creating a business plan is an **absolute must**:

Obtaining a Business Loan – The majority of business start-ups will require a business loan to get off the ground. These loans are used pay for initial business costs, such as supplies, marketing costs, labor, upfront payments and support resources. Existing businesses can more easily take out a loan to pay for the resources necessary to expand their business. However, you just can't walk into a bank and expect to walk out with a loan, on the strength of your word alone! Most banks will require you to present your plan to a bank officer who will then determine if your plan is worth investing in. A solid business plan will show the bank officer that you're committed to keeping your business afloat and profitable.

Seeking Investors – An investor is a person who provides upfront capital to a business in the anticipation of gaining a monetary return when the business is successfully up and running. While investors are similar to bank loans, the main difference is that investors don't require you to repay your debt on a predetermined schedule, as would a bank. At the same time, just as a bank officer won't give you a loan on demand without a plan to back it up, neither will an investor. If you cannot demonstrate solid prospects of a positive outcome in your financial projections, an investor will not be inclined to put up any money toward your business.

Separating Dream from Reality – In the beginning of a new business, it is easy to let your emotions run rampant in everything from your passions to your visions. Your emotions may be so powerful that they cause you to think too big too quickly. While it's not a bad thing to have big long-term vision, it is even more important to have your feet firmly planted in reality. A well-developed business plan can force you to step into what is real right now and can help you focus on the next right thing to do. In addition, whenever your emotions cause you to start doubting yourself and your abilities, a quick review of the foundations of your business plan can help to banish those negative thoughts!

Selling Your Business – Although you may put hours and hours of hard work, passion and dedication into your business, don't let your identity become tied to it. the most valuable piece of advice I've ever received as a business owner is this: <u>don't become emotionally attached to your business</u>. Launching a business, bringing it to successful maturity, and then selling it is actually a very strategic business move. It's a great way to make money without having to work the rest of your life away. However, your business will never have any buyers without a business plan. Potential buyers will want to see why your business is worth buying; they want to see its present value and – more importantly – its future potential. All this is bound up in your business plan.

Building Your Team – Unless you're a sole proprietor, it's likely that you're going to need a team of at least a few people to help you with your venture. A well-thought-out business plan can show potential team members that your business is serious; it can also inspire them to work hard and can focus them on what is most important to your success. A great business plan can attract high-quality talent, which can make a huge difference in your ultimate business success.

Consulting with Your Allies – As a business owner, you should always have a team that consists of a banker, an accountant, a lawyer and possibly a business coach or consultant if you're a first-timer. Bankers can help you with much more than getting a loan. They can help you choose payroll options, provide discounted banking services to your employees, and even provide insurance options, just to mention a few services.

An accountant can handle your business taxes and advise you regarding finances, both of which are essential to keeping a business afloat. A lawyer may not seem necessary at first glance, but having one is very important. A lawyer can point you in the right direction when it comes to handling business legalities and can offer you solid advice on the best way to expand your business, especially when the time comes to build an online presence. You'd be surprised at all the legal business requirements you know nothing about! The rules and regulations can be very confusing, especially since they often differ by state. A lawyer can help you stay out of hot water if you ever run into a liability issue.

Finally, you can benefit greatly from having a business coach, someone who can help you learn to become a master entrepreneur. A business plan will make it much easier for these support people to do their jobs. It will also help ensure that everybody is on the same page, when it comes to supporting your pursuit of your goals.

Resource Planning – A business plan can help you project your financial needs, especially when it comes to fixed costs. It is reckless to make unnecessarily large purchases or hire too many employees if you don't have the means to support them. In some situations, it makes more sense to rent office space, as opposed to buying it. These are the sort of resource constraints the finance section of your business plan can help clarify.

Catching Errors Early – When you create a business plan, you'll have everything about your business written out right in front of you. This means that it will be easier to catch big errors early on in the process. For example, if part of your sales goal is to produce 5,000 widgets by the end of each month, yet your resource planning section only calls for one employee to work on the production line, it's more than likely that you will have a very hard time reaching that goal. It's better to realize this before you throw your one and only employee into an unrealistic situation! A business plan is something you can easily scan to see the big picture and catch expectations that don't mesh with the reality of your resources.

Proving to Yourself You Can Do It – Most importantly, a business plan proves to yourself that you can actually do it! Starting a business, especially for the first time, can be an overwhelming task. Your business plan can put everything in perspective for you.

As soon as you have a completed document, you'll be more likely to feel empowered to do what needs doing! Your business plan will enable you to feel confident about the projected success of your business. The ability to intimately describe the inner workings of your business is an extremely powerful motivator.

The basics of business planning can easily be described by answering the traditional "who, what, where when, how and why" questions:

Who Needs a Business Plan?

Anyone and everyone who wants to start a new business will need a plan if they want to be successful. As I mentioned earlier, you don't *have* to sit down and design a plan, but by failing to do so, your chances of failure will be dramatically increased. A business plan helps you define and manage your business mission and goals, clarify marketing strategies and define target audience information, manage your finances and set up the company's structure. If you do not have all that information together in a place where your entire team can refer to it, your business is likely to fail.

Goal-setting

First and foremost, a business plan helps you define your company goals. Setting goals and objectives for your business is a standard part of the planning process; it will form the backbone of your business's success. Its objectives are your overall intentions for the business; the goals express how you plan to get there. Once your business reaches one goal, it can then reach toward something even bigger and better.

You can always create goals in your head or even jot them down on scraps of paper, but in both cases, they are easily misplaced or forgotten. However, when you state them as part of your business plan, you will not only have easy access reference to them but they become integrated with the rest of your efforts to make a go of the business.

Goals are so much more than just statements. To successfully reach your goals, it is usually necessary to spend time with them. Write them out in detail and then break them down into smaller, manageable steps that you can easily bang out in order to accomplish the final outcome. At the same time, your goals are not stand-alone statements; they should always be shaped in support of your overall business purpose. This purpose is defined in your vision and mission statements.

Vision and Mission Statements

The process of conceiving and ultimately describing your vision and mission statement is just as important as goal setting. A company's vision is a compass; it marks where the company is headed, both in general terms and in specific stages. A small, home-based business can grow into a successful, well-known corporation, but only with a clearly stated vision and mission statement upon which to build strategies and goals.

Giving your business a vision will help fuel your goals and motivate you and your team to move your company forward, from something small to something incredible. A mission statement helps you define your target audience, making it easier to ultimately reel in potential customers increase your profits.

Mission statements often promote the greater good, thereby appealing to specific customers. For example, a grocery store whose mission is to help conserve the environment would most likely appeal to customers who eat organic produce. This would secure a solid profit base, because organic produce usually has greater profit margins than non-organic products.

12

Goal: Provide excellent customer service when meeting with mobile Notary to provide vision.

mission: customers that Req a Notary Public at their business or home.

A business plan can help you clearly define the product or service you are offering to consumers. One of the first sections in your plan requires you to describe your product/service in great detail, including the reason you're selling it, an explanation of how it matches up to the competition, and its projected list price.

A business plan helps you define your target audience and describe an ideal client profile the company can use to locate that ideal customer in the real world. Knowing your target audience is one of the most important factors in determining the success of a business.

An old friend of mine, Helene, was a business coach who was looking to develop her clientele, increase her leads, and make her business more profitable. When I was younger, I interned for her as a business development director; in this capacity, I helped her find fresh ways to generate leads. I quickly noticed that she didn't have a well-defined business development strategy; this was preventing her from being able to clearly define her ideal client. When I asked her to describe her target audience, she replied "Everybody, everywhere."

Since Helene's business was largely remote, she thought it didn't matter who or from where she got her leads. However, the answer "everybody, everywhere" encompasses more than 7 billion people, from 24 different time zones, speaking a host of languages. This answer does nothing to define a realistic customer base.

Over time, however, I was able to help her narrow down her answer to "overwhelmed business owners in the Rhode Island area." Since she was a business coach, her audience was obviously business owners and since she lived in Rhode Island, we decided it would be easier for her to focus in on that area, for the time being. Using descriptions of her last few clients, we were able quickly and easily to put together an ideal client profile that would help us properly target similar clients who were more likely to say, "yes" to her business.

Keep in mind that it's not uncommon for companies to actually shift their target audience partway into their run. The Kellogg Company is a great example of this. In the beginning, Kellogg's target audience for their breakfast cereals was children. However, their market share fell dramatically in the early 1980s. Instead of allowing the company to cave, the executives refocused their target audience, focusing on baby-boomers. To appeal to this audience they began to emphasize the importance of eating a balanced breakfast. This caused the company to bounce right back to the top of the breakfast cereal industry.

Define Your Business Structure

A business plan can also help you describe the structure of your company. In your plan, you can describe the legal structure of your business, identify your business leaders, and discuss the flow of your business. You will also note if your business requires any special licenses or permits in order to operate.

Flex Within Your Identity

Having a business plan in place is more important now than ever before. The life of businesses today largely depends on responding to trends that are constantly changing, thanks to the burgeoning rate of information consumers receive on a daily basis. Only when you have a clearly defined identity anchored in the marketplace are you able to adjust your positioning in order to take advantage of shifts in customer preferences.

For example, McDonalds started out as a fast food restaurant that primarily served hamburgers and French fries. While they're best known for their original menu, times have changed; now many consumers are more interested in eating healthy food. Let's face it – when you're trying to eat healthier, McDonald's isn't the first restaurant that comes to mind!.

So, how did McDonald's respond? They responded to the market trends by adding healthier menu choices. Salads, grilled chicken wraps, and unsweetened beverages all made an appearance. If

McDonalds had stuck to their original menu and ignored the trends, would they still be regarded as one of the top fast food chains today? Probably not. Instead, they would be remembered with nostalgia as a has-been.

Grow Within Your Identity

A business plan can also help you manage business growth. Let's use McDonald's again as an example. The golden arches got its start with one restaurant in California. A man named Ray Kroc had a vision, which led him to grab up the McDonald's brand when it came up for sale. He then opened several locations, which then quickly spiraled into hundreds that eventually spanned the globe.

Let's pretend for a minute that McDonald's was not the huge success that it is today. Instead, let's say the brand was a huge failure, but Ray Kroc didn't know it because he didn't have an adequate business plan. When the brand began to spread just across the United States, it wouldn't have been able to stand under the weight of the additional stores. However, having a business plan that allows for growth and greater profitability is most likely a huge reason McDonalds now has restaurants all around the world.

Plan a Firm Financial Footing

Finally, a business plan can help you manage the finances of your business and of your related products/services. A properly written financials section should give anyone who reads your business plan a clear understanding of your business's financial projections and abilities. The financial plan usually includes a balance sheet, an income statement, and a cash flow statement.

Why Do You Need a Business Plan?

You need a business plan because it enables you to easily manage your business without becoming overwhelmed, confused, or disorganized. Your plan will contain all the basic information about your business for partners, potential investors, and advisors to draw on. It helps you focus on what's important and gives you a basis from which to adjust to the winds of change. A business plan can help you attract potential investors and eventually buyers, if and when you are ready to sell your successful venture.

It is incredibly easy to learn the process. Anyone can do it. Since a business plan gives you a much higher chance of making it past the two year mark, there's truly no reason *not* to have one!

What Type of Business Plan is Right for You?

What comes to mind when you imagine what a business plan looks like? I personally envision a sleek, typed document, housed in a fancy cover that is stored in a company's secret vault. Others may picture a simple online document that is easy to edit and update as the business grows and develops. Yet others may visualize a handwritten notebook full of business details and sketches.

There really is no right answer as to what a business plan looks like. However, there are several **types** of plans you can design. The type of plan that is best for your business often depends on multiple factors, such as the business's size, the company's primary focus, etc.

There are two basic types of business plans. **Formal** business plans are usually typed, detailed documents that are often intended as a tool to secure funding. **Informal** business plans, on the other hand, focus more on a company's goals and are often handwritten and less strictly organized. Although you can easily handwrite a business plan, I recommend creating a computer-based document, even if it's intended to be informal. Regardless of the size of your business, even an informal business plan is more easily accessed, updated and organized.

Within these two categories are a few more types of business plans. These are each based on a specific purpose:

- **Feasibility Plans:** Feasibility plans are used to measure the practical possibility of making a profit from a business's product or service. These plans will describe the product or service, identify the target audience and the need you hope to meet, an accounting for the necessary capital, followed by recommendations for moving ahead.

  Before you jump into *any* business venture, I recommend you write up a basic feasibility study for your product or service. After all, you need to know if it will be worth all the effort of putting in on the market – that is, unless you've already put it out there just for the heck of it and have "accidentally" stumbled upon success, like my friend Denise!

  Unfortunately, while your product or service may seem like a genius idea to you and your friends, you need to know if it also sounds like a genius idea to the people out there who will buy it – your audience – your customers. Many people make the mistake of not researching this practicality and quickly go under when they discover the hard way that they can't make a profit. You've got to be reasonably certain of the market demand for your product. Otherwise, you're writing a recipe for failure.

  You may also find feasibility plans helpful for when you want to introduce additional products or services into the market. Many existing companies will give a new product a test run just to see how it is received. If they find it successful, it can easily be added to the company's product or service offering.

- **Startup Plans:** Start-up plans are designed for when you're envisioning or just beginning a new business. Hopefully, you will have completed your own feasibility studies and these will be included in your startup plan.
  Start-up plans lay out the basics of your business, including your company description, your product or service description, the configuration of your management team,

a market analysis, and a financial analysis. You can easily form a basic start-up plan with limited knowledge; then you can customize your plan as your business needs develop.

- **Strategic Plans:** Strategic plans take a closer and much more detailed look at a company's goals, so that the entire business can benefit, continue to profit, and can progress the top 25%. A proper strategic plan should include your company's vision and mission statements and will lay out critical success factors, including goals, strategies that will be employed to reach those goals, and a proposed timeline for reaching them. As your business begins grow, you will find yourself coming back to this document repeatedly to follow up on your goals, look for areas of improvement, and to set down new goals that will keep your business flourishing in the black. You can also easily include these items in your start-up plan

- **Growth Plans:** Growth plans focus on a company's proposed development and how to manage growth successfully. Growth plans can be written for internal or external purposes. The information in a growth plan will vary but it will often be written to address specific potential investors. For this reason, a growth plan will include a highly detailed description of the company and its key players, as well as a clear description of present financial status and projected expansion markets and expected revenues, based upon anticipated demand.

- **Internal Audience Plans:** Internal audience plans are used by existing businesses to describe and promote a specific project. Internal audience plans describe to all the parties involved the details of the proposed project, where your company currently stands in terms of profitability, and where it wants to go. They help a business determine how much money it will need to put out in support of the project and will detail the cost of each project resource. It will also outline possible marketing tactics that will support the project. These plans often include a market analysis to show where the company stands in relationship to its competition.

- **Operational Plans:** Operational plans are written in the same way as internal audience plans except that they focus on how your business operates. For example, if your company wants to reach a specific deadline for introducing a new product or service, those details would be laid out in this kind of plan. Again, first-time business owners will not need to worry about utilizing this type of plan until their company has developed into a much larger entity.

When is the Best Time to Create a Business Plan?

The truth is, once you've started to seriously visualize your business, you've already begun creating a business plan in your head. Yet, your business can't become a reality until you physically put it down in black and white. It's a simple task, but it stops many people cold.

Over the years, hundreds of individuals have come to me, asking if I could help them start a business. The first actionable task I give them is to develop a business plan and then report back to me when it's written down. So far, I've not heard back from a single person. That's because the sheer process of creating an actual business plan can be scary indeed.

Suddenly this dream of yours takes shape in reality and that, my friend, can unleash all sorts of emotions! Fear can overwhelm you, self-doubt can rise up to assail you; you may even begin to question your sanity for daring to imagine that you could create this, this *thing*. However, if you can fight through these emotions to set down even the most basic plan, you will have overcome a major obstacle to your success. After all, you will have made it further than everyone *else* who has asked me for help!

There's really no standard entrepreneurial answer as to when to create your business plan. My opinion is that as soon as you can envision your business, you should write down a plan. As I mentioned earlier, you may have a GREAT idea for a product or service, but once you begin researching the market, you could discover that it's really not all that unique and there's no demand for it, setting you back to square one. Yet, that could be your salvation, because it will have prevented you from wasting time and effort in the pursuit of failure!

The *best* time to find out that your product or service will work – or not work – like you envisioned it, is now. The sooner you create your plan, the earlier you will know if it will work. Also, the earlier you lay out your plan, the more committed you will be to getting your business up and running. We're like that, you know. We tend to be more committed if we have skin in the game. The more sweat you invest into your project, the more determined you will become to see it succeed.

If you have an idea but keep putting off developing a business plan for it, your business will never get off the ground. It'll just continue to float around in nebulous form as a mere pipe dream.

You want to write your business plan now, while your business is in its infancy. If you wait until your business is a full-fledged concern, you will have already developed systems that are so complex that they are difficult to tease out onto paper. It's much better to define your business as it is in its simplest form. Then, as you establish and adjust the systems and processes, you can note them down as you grow. In this way, your plan will grow and develop along with your business.

How Do I Write a Business Plan?

There are many ways to get started on the creation of your business plan. I know many people who have simply researched what a business plan should contain and then just put all of that information together into a document. There are hundreds of business plan templates available on the internet. It's also quite possible to outsource the job; some business owners hire writers to get their business plans written.

As you progress through this book, you'll learn to create your own business plan by following straightforward step-by-step instructions. Starting in a couple of chapters, I will begin to walk you through the details of each part of your plan, a section at a time. By the end of this book, if you do the work as you read, you will have your very first business plan finished and ready to go!

Chapter 2: Common Mistakes People Make and How to Avoid Them

While there are many important details you should pay attention to when creating your business plan, there are also some things that you should avoid doing at all costs. Some of these simple mistakes can cost you big time. Even a small mistake or two can cause you to lose potential investors. Some errors can send you careening into major roadblocks, partway down the road; these are usually issues which, had you seen them coming, you would have been able to deal with them before they grew into huge boulders. Knowing how to identify and avoid these mistakes up front can save you the hassle of starting all over again partway through the process.

Purchasing Business Software – There are free computer programs and other apps that can assist you in creating a business plan. Your favorite word processor will do quite nicely, however. As this book progresses, you'll learn how to easily create your own template, using your favorite word-processing application. For a start-up plan, there's no need to sink money into complicated software.

Including Too Much Written Text – While your business plan should include important information in written form, you don't need to write down *everything*. Since business plans are meant to be short and to the point, excessive text can muddy, rather than clarify, the waters. As you develop your draft, ask yourself which information is the most important to communicate. Focus on putting down the factual information clearly and succinctly, keeping in mind that you will have an opportunity to verbally communicate your passion for your work in person, whenever you present the plan to others.

Ignoring Weaknesses and Possible Pitfalls – When you're writing a business plan, it is only normal that you'll want to focus on highlighting your business's strengths. At the same time, you don't want to ignore possible weaknesses. While you shouldn't put *too* much emphasis on this, it is still important to describe potential points of weakness in your business and describe how you plan to address them. Doing so allows you to prioritize your biggest risks and prepare contingency plans that allow you to face them with confidence. Your preparation will not only equip you, but will also relieve any anxiety on the part of potential investors and partners.

Over-planning – Yes, planning is essential to business success – but over-planning can be dangerous. In all your planning and contingency preparation, give yourself enough room to breathe. While it's important to anticipate future "what ifs," and know how to prepare for contingencies, don't waste excessive time planning for something with a slim probability of occurring.

Risk assessment, however, is another item entirely. Risk planning is a practice borrowed from the field of project management. Project managers often brainstorm to uncover possible, impossible, and even vaguely probable risks. They then evaluate these risks in terms of severity of impact and probability of occurrence. Only then do they turn their attention to developing contingency plans for the risks that are most impactful and most likely to occur.

Let's say that you're creating a business plan to open a fast food franchise. In doing this, there are plenty of "what if's" to consider: what if my competitor opens up a store right across the street? What if my competitor drastically expands her menu? What if a new health trend develops? I'm sure you'll get the idea.

Here's how you can face each of these question.

What If My Competitor Drastically Expands Her Menu?

While it is possible to be a little behind in menu offerings, it is important to remember that menu expansion won't occur overnight. First, the company will go through the process of acquiring funding and approval at the corporate level to add new products to their lineup. Then it's likely that the corporation will release the new items to a limited test market to see how well they sell before releasing them on a company-wide level. All of that takes time on your competitor's end. If the company you're franchising for does the same, it will take time on your end as well. Though it may slightly affect your sales if this does happen, it's probably not anything you can control, so you shouldn't worry about factoring it into your initial plan

What If My Competitor Opens A Store Right Across The Street?

For this question, the first thing you should consider is real estate. Are you operating in a rural area where businesses are few and far between? Are you operating in an urban area where there's a vacant storefront on every corner? If you're operating in an area where you're not surrounded by open land or open real estate, than this worry would most likely be low on the priority list. However, if you're operating on a busy thoroughfare where businesses are popping up left and right, then this concern may be worth considering. It may even warrant creating a contingency plan at some point.

What If A New Health Trend Develops?

As we all know, every year there's a new health trend that causes consumers to modify their diets. A question like this may have a high probability of occurring, but its possible impact on you depends on the nature of your business. If you run a vegan joint or a vegetarian-based restaurant, you may not have to worry about these health trends at all, since you're already addressing them. If your franchise serves up nothing but greasy fried foods, on the other hand, you may want to consider developing a contingency plan that will encourage consumers to continue giving you their business

The most important thing to remember is that your plan is a living document, open to adjustment, as the conditions warrant. At this stage in the game, asking too many "what ifs" can be a distraction from what is most important – getting your business plan finished and moving forward to get your business launched!

Remember It's About Your Business

One mistake that many first-time business owners make is that their plan will revolve too much around their product or service and not the business itself. While it is important to know your product or service inside out, it is important to keep in mind that your product or service is likely to change once it's made available to consumers. Your business will be the more systematic entity. Therefore, it is important to remember that your business should be the center of attention in your plan and not just your product or service.

Of course, you can (and I encourage you to) create a separate plan to flesh out the details of what you'll be selling. This may even be a good idea before you go to begin your business plan so you have the excitement of your product or service out of your system. The best way to approach this is to make the execution of your business your main priority. One of the biggest and most important parts of execution is time and money. Business owners who do not do well often fail to plan for allocating time and money when they have to change something about their product or service or even their marketing strategy.

Sloppy, Informal Writing

One thing you don't want to do is present a sloppy, poorly-written plan that is riddled with spelling and grammatical errors. Although you're not writing your business plan for an Honors English class, potential investors will be put off by a poorly-written plan. The structure you use for your plan isn't nearly as important such as your spelling and grammar. However, this is a problem that is fairly simple to fix. You can easily hire a skilled editor online to correct your errors and even to improve the structure of your logic.

I can't ensure that your spelling and grammar are perfect as is, but I can help you see that each section is well-organized and that it sends a strong positive message to your readers. As you read ahead, feel free to borrow liberally from my instructions.

Trying to Finish in One Day

It's next to impossible to finish your plan within one day so don't even consider it as a goal! The start of a new business plan usually requires several days to think through and sketch out on paper, before even writing the first draft.

Your business plan is important enough that you don't want to rush through the process. At the same time, because it's a living document you'll never actually be "finished" with it. Let yourself work on this over the course of a week or two, writing a section and then setting it aside to review later for consistency and accuracy. Often, in the rereading, you will be able to pick out things that don't make sense, or logic that just doesn't work.

Waiting Too Long To Start

On the other hand, don't wait too long to begin creating your plan. If you have a great business idea in your head, start setting it down on paper as soon as possible. You don't have to write out a full-blown plan, but you can at least start sketching out your ideas. Then you can flesh it out further as you continue to think things through.

Presenting an Incomplete Plan

This point is a bit of a no-brainer but I am including it because I know how easy it is to
fall into this trap, especially for first-time entrepreneurs. The whole business planning process can seem like a painful, unnecessary step, especially when you're super-excited about your business and you're raring to dive right into the market and start selling. However, please don't let your enthusiasm lead you into skipping over parts of the business plan.

First, investors and other professionals won't even give you a second thought if you haven't done the proper market research, haven't fleshed out your company description, or haven't included some of the sections you're soon going to learn about. Secondly, an incomplete business plan will not be able to guide you through the start-up process, nor will it help you stay on track if your business *does* succeed and begins to grow. You'll find yourself playing catch-up so you'll be able to move forward, all the while you're juggling the existing business.

Of course, I don't think you'll have to worry about creating an incomplete plan, because you're reading this book! Of course you're going to follow through with each chapter, completing each section of your business plan as you go along! However, there's always somebody in the bunch who'll want to jump ahead without giving much thought to their plan. Let me warn you now…don't.

Keeping it all in your Head

I know many entrepreneurial-minded people who can easily visualize their visions and lay out everything in their head, but trust me on this one: keeping your plan in your head is never a good idea! Being a business owner can be very demanding, making it difficult to remember small details from your plan and it's crucial to know your plan inside-out, especially for your financial projections! There wouldn't be anything worse than having a financial mess-up because you got a number or two wrong from your memory.

On that note, don't be tempted to create your plan by hand, either. Even though we live in a technological age, I still know many people who like to keep handwritten notes, journals, folders, etc. I favor handwriting over typing myself but I can tell you from experience that keeping a digital is the way to go. Of course, your business plan may start out in a notebook as a few handwritten pages of notes, and that's okay, but it is likely that those notes will expand and the easiest way to track changes is by using a word processor

Worrying About the Size of Your Plan

That being said, don't worry about the actual size of your plan. There's no set rule for its length. What matters most is the substance and quality of your plan. You could have a 100-page plan but if your marketing and financial information is poorly researched, no amount of writing will help your business survive. An amazing business plan could be short but still include the excellent research, well thought out marketing and financial strategies and all the essential information that that a business plan should include

Relying on Quantitative Statistics

While it is important to include some quantitative statistics in your plan, potential investors will likely want to see more organic research, such as statistics from prospective customers themselves. You should already have a good idea of what your target audiences looks like, so don't be afraid to interview potential customers who fall into that demographic and include what they have to say in your research. Science is only powerful to a certain extent, but when investors, potential partners, employees, and others see that you've gone out and have started making moves with actual customers, they are much more likely to feel confident in your business's ability to succeed

Using Jargon Without Explanations

Since you are likely an expert in the industry in which you will be conducting business, it may be natural to fall into this trap. The people, who will read your plan, however, probably won't know what you're talking about unless you explain yourself. One of the purposes of a business plan is to provide an easy snapshot of your business; using unfamiliar jargon takes the word "easy" out of that description. You can still use all the technical jargon you want, but explain it so that anyone who reads your plan will understand what you're trying to say.

Sloppy Financial Projections

One mistake many first time business owners make is to come up short on financial projections. Your best source of information can be similar businesses that are already out there. You can easily research organizations to learn their average operating costs. If you can't find what you're looking for online, you can always turn to an expert to help you out. For example, my friend's, uncle owns a seafood restaurant and Michael, my friend, was looking into opening his own steakhouse. It was natural for him to look to his uncle for guidance on operating costs, like facility overhead, workers' wages, kitchen equipment, dining room equipment, etc. Michael was fortunate to have someone nearby he could turn to, but if that's not possible for you, another option is networking. Most states have entrepreneurial organizations that are more than willing to help you out by providing guidance and mentorship. They usually have networking meetings where you can rub shoulders with local people in your field. You can also always turn to LinkedIn for professional advice. Don't forget about your professional contacts – your banker, lawyer, or accountant can often answer questions about business-related costs, and make suggestions regarding insurance options, banking options, business structure costs, etc.

Ignoring Constructive Criticism

Nobody wants to hear anyone say anything bad about their amazingly genius business idea, but don't close your mind to feedback. Accept that you are too close to your baby to be objective about it and keep yourself open to ideas, even those that are contrary to what you want to hear. Avoid filtering out possible pitfalls, roadblocks and other challenges others may be interested in talking about. By showing your plan to others and listening to their advice, you can be apprised easily of things you may have missed entirely or will need to revisit. Doing this before you present it to more important players, can increase your probabilities of success.

As you can tell, most of these common mistakes are pretty simple and you can easily avoid them once you know to be on the lookout. Now, let's look at the process of developing your business plan and how you can facilitate your progress.

Chapter 3: Beginning the Planning Process

One of the first things you can do to smooth the road ahead of you is to create a comfortable working environment. If you're already a skilled writer, you probably already know how to do this so feel free to skip this section and go right to the next step. However, if you've never done much writing, you might want to consider this advice.

As a writer, I find that my environment can have a huge impact on my success. I can't concentrate on my writing when the TV is on or music is playing in the background, at least not music that isn't designed to help me concentrate. I simply can't concentrate on my inner words when other people are being loud and distracting. Similarly, I find it hard to concentrate when I'm sitting at my kitchen table instead of my office, where I have much adequate lighting and appropriate seating. I've also learned that if I don't shut off my favorite social media sites, I'll be frequently distracted by notifications, especially when I'm in the middle of pouring out my latest, most brilliant ideas! Everybody has their own prime distractions; I'm sure you'll discover yours soon enough, if you haven't already.

There are several things you can do to create an ideal writing environment, one that will help your process run smoothly. Again, we can use the "who, what, where, when" process to make these tips easy to remember.

Who?

Who should be present when you're writing? You'll need yourself, of course. You're the person who knows everything about the business. If you're going into business with a someone else, you may need your partner to help you draft the plan. Your partner need not be present for the actual writing, but should be included in the review of key points before you write, to check portions for accuracy during the writing, and to evaluate the completed draft and ensure that the plan is complete and correct.

What?

What do you need to begin writing? You'll need your computer, of course, and any research you've compiled, along with notes you've put together. You'll need this book for reference, along with any online templates you choose to utilize.

You'll want to keep yourself hydrated, so keep a bottle of water handy and remind yourself to take a sip every few minutes. Some people like to keep snacks on their desk. Personally, I would be munching constantly if I kept snacks within reach, so I don't need the temptation. I prefer to use the urge for a snack as an impetus to get me up out of my chair and move around for a bit; it refreshes the brain and keeps atrophy from setting in completely!

Speaking of chairs, you want to sit in one that's comfortable and supportive enough that you won't be distracted by aching muscles. If you don't have an official desk chair, you can easily modify a regular chair by adding pillows or even purchasing ergonomic supports, whatever you need to create something you can sit in for an extended time. I use a swivel chair and have taught myself the fine art of fidgeting; it's a wonderful way to burn some energy while you're seated, and yet keep yourself alert.

Sometimes I get bored with my location and decide I need some variety. Fortunately, I have a laptop so it's a simple matter to grab my charging cord, pack things up, and relocate to another room or even outside, if the weather is nice. Some writers venture further afield, doing their work in restaurants, coffee shops, or public libraries. It's really up to you to choose the environment in which you work best.

You'll want to pay attention to the sensory input offered by your environment. Music can help you focus; if you are working in a room with distracting noises, a set of noise-cancelling headphones can be a wonderful investment. Even a pair of earbuds, streaming the right kind of instrumental music (lyrics will conflict with the words in your head) can help you focus. At times, I've used aromatherapy to help me concentrate. I often light a fragrant candle or burn some incense to focus my attention within the bubble of the fragrance when I'm getting ready to write.

There are also some things you *don't* want around when you're preparing to write your plan. If you're as easily distracted by your phone as I am, that's the first thing that should go. Turn your ringer down and leave your phone in another room so you're not tempted to check it every five minutes. I will leave my phone in the room with me, but will turn it face down; I'll often set it behind me or far enough away that I have to get up to grab it.

If you're easily distracted by social media websites, you can use a webpage-blocking app to block your social media websites. Most web browsers have built-in blocking functions under their privacy settings but the apps are much more flexible, allowing you greater control of what you block and when you block it. A quick online search can pull up dozens of free website blockers.

As tempting as radio and TV can be, I recommended turning them off while you're writing. You can always record your favorite shows and go back to them later or just write before or after they air. I do, at times, use television as a form of mental distraction. If my mind starts to churn, working on solving a particular problem, or if I'm starting to tire from the sheer complexity of what I'm working on, I'll use the natural magnetism of the television as a way to give my brain a break for a few minutes. After a set time, I'll turn the television off and return to my work with a refreshed mind that is better able to tackle the challenges I'm facing.

When?

When should you write? This answer varies for everyone based on their personal preferences. I once worked alongside a man who woke up at 4 a.m. every day to write, because he thrived in the morning and had the whole house to himself at that hour. Some people find it better to write late at night, after they've settled down from a long day. If you're not sure when your best time to thrive at writing is, take a few days to experiment and see for yourself when you are at your creative best.

Where?

Where should you write? Again, this is a question that depends on personal preference. I recommend finding a nice, quiet place where you can relax and concentrate. Unless you have ultimate willpower, I don't recommend writing in your living room, bedroom, or kitchen, because those areas contain all sorts of distractions and are prone to more traffic. If you can't work at home, your neighborhood library will usually provide a quiet environment with minimal distractions. You can use your own laptop, but most libraries also provide computers for use.

Once you've decided where and when you're going to write your business plan, the second step is to make sure that you have gathered all the research you will need before you begin. It can be helpful to create your template in a new word document before you start. To easily create your own simple template, open up a new word document, name it appropriately and then starting with chapter 4 of this book, copy each chapter title onto a new page in the document until you've got them all. Then you'll want to begin researching your business idea and its industry.

If you've already researched your business idea in depth then you can go ahead and skip this step. However, if you're still in the "idea" phase and haven't given your idea much thought in terms of reality, then this section can help you.

The best way to research your business idea is to look at it from different perspectives. Look at it from the perspective of the business owner, look at it from the perspective of your consumers and look at it from the perspective of your competitors. A great way to break all of this down is to perform a **SWOT Analysis**. A SWOT Analysis is a diagram that can create a snapshot of your business's strengths, weaknesses, opportunities and threats. The best way to construct this diagram is to create a grid with four squares and designate each square for each category. Under the strengths category, you can list all of the strengths that you have identified about your business and in the weakness category, list all of the potential flaws and risks. In the opportunities category, you can list ideas that may present opportunities to your business, such as health trends, lifestyle trends, target market changes, etc. Under the threats category, you can list any ideas that may pose as threats to your business, such as competitors' moves, the economy, state and federal-mandated pricing, etc. Performing a SWOT analysis can be especially helpful for ranking and prioritizing risks and threats so that you can determine whether you can control them and if it's worth creating a contingency plan.

It's also a good idea to perform some industry research before you get into your more in-depth market research. Industry research may be a little challenging at first, especially if you've never done it before, but you will be surprised about how much info is actually out there. It will require some patience and some experimentation. Depending on what your industry is, sometimes it will be as simple as typing in "[your industry] statistics" and finding almost all of the information you need. Sometimes you won't be able to find any information by doing it that way. Before starting to research your industry, I recommend creating a list of questions about your industry so you know the specific answers that you're looking for.

A good place to begin is with the Department of Labor's Bureau of Labor Statistics website (https://www.bls.gov/). Here, you can research your industry and find information pertaining to regional consumer pricing, employment costs, unemployment statistics and median income statistics, industry outlook information and economic information. Another valuable source of information are through industry organizations. The Directory of Associations (http://www.directoryofassociations.com/) is a great place to begin looking for an association in your industry and in your state. Other great places to try are industry trade shows, industry magazines, LinkedIn, online industry guides and of course library references. You may also find some published books and reports about your industry.

Chapter 4: Writing Your Executive Summary

Although the executive summary is the first thing that I will teach you how to write, you'll actually have to revisit this chapter because it is important to save its creation for last. An executive summary is just what it's called – a concise, one-page summary of what your business plan contains. A good rule of thumb is to make the length of your executive summary 10% of the length of your entire document.

Sometimes, potential investors will *only* read your executive summary to determine whether they want to invest their resources into a new business. The main goal for new business owners is to persuade and the main challenge is to do it in as few words as possible – sometimes only several sentences! Businesses that are already up and running may use an executive summary to describe growth strategies, updated goals or to acquire extra financing. This chapter will focus on how you can write a great executive summary for a startup business.

A proper executive summary should include an introduction of yourself, your business, and your product or service. It will also summarize key advantages that will make your business successful and do so in the least amount of words possible. it is extremely important that you choose the words in your executive summary carefully; they are what will sell your idea to potential investors.

This section must include the following information:

The Need – Briefly explain how your business will fulfil a need in the lives of your target audience.

The Strategy – Briefly explain how you will offer your products or services to your target audience.

The Audience – Provide an informative snapshot of your targeted customer demographic.

The Structure – Provide a description of your product or service and explain why your target audience will want to buy from you.

The Sales – Briefly explain your sales and marketing strategy.

The Enemy – Provide a brief description of your competition and explain where your business has a competitive edge.

The Dollars – Provide a brief snapshot of financial information pertaining to your business, as well as a financial projection showing at least three years into the future.

The Profiles – Briefly introduce yourself and any other partners as well as employees or team members and what they bring to your business.

The Schedule – Provide a schedule of events that shows how you will move your business from its initial creation to its actual functioning.

If you are looking for an investor, or you want to borrow money from an institution, you can include that information in your executive summary as well. Briefly note how much money you will need and state how much equity your potential investors would receive back.

Keep in mind that investors and institutions won't yield up their money immediately after reading your executive summary. While it's important for them to know what kind of financing you're looking for and what they can get in return, the main goal is move those representatives to the point that they want to meet with you and discuss your business. *That* will be the place where you can really reel them in.

As usual, there are certain things that you should **not** include in your executive summary, including:

Clichés – Avoid using overused and exaggerated terms that investors and institutions see regularly on most of the executive summaries they read. Capture your audience with simple but straightforward, precise, and confident language.

Technical Jargon – Again, the people reading your executive summary will likely be investors who won't be conversant your field's technical jargon. Industry-related technical terms, especially acronyms and abbreviations, can confuse and distract from the true intent of your summary. To ensure that your executive summary is easy to understand, write it for a ten year old. If a child can understand what you're saying then you know an adult will be able to understand it.

Missing Info – Don't omit key information about your management team and prospective employees. Even if a person thinks your concept is strong and your product will be a winner, potential funders are unlikely to commit unless they can see you have a solid management structure, a well-thought-through plan of operations, and a team of respected advisors you are committed to listening to.

Ghostwriters – Whatever you do, don't hire a ghostwriter to create your executive summary. Although it may seem like a pain, after having already created the entire document, it is important that you write this yourself, for several reasons. Writing the executive summary yourself enables you to see if you've forgotten to include any key research or accidentally omitted a key piece of information. Writing this summary yourself will help cement the whole plan in your brain and will make it easier to formulate your own presentations. The process of condensing your entire plan into a brief summary will help you focus on what is most important when it comes to the actual creation of your business.

If you're not sure how to get started, or afraid that your executive summary will turn out to be too long, go back through your business plan and pick out up to two sentences that summarizes each section. Use these to formulate your executive summary. Read it back to yourself out loud to ensure that it makes sense and then ask a friend or family member to read it to ensure that it's understandable and answers all questions that investors or banks may ask. It is helpful to break your executive summary into sections with headings. This makes it easier for readers to read quickly and skim it if they need to pick out specific items.

A Sample Executive Summary

Here is an example of a good executive summary for a fictional freelance writing business:

"Writers United is a startup company that will provide high quality yet affordable freelance writing services to business coaches in the Tri-State area. Writers United is scheduled to begin operation on January 1, 2018 and will be run as a single-member LLC by John Smith, former head writer for The Daily Press.

"Writers United will provide original written material to business coaches in New York, New Jersey and Pennsylvania for marketing purposes. Its target will be busy male business coaches who lack the necessary time and/or skills to produce their own written material. There are currently 100,000 business coaches in the Tri-State area, 75% of whom are males and are likely to outsource written material. The projected growth rate for business coaches is 5%.

"Writers United will provide its services through remote connections between writer John Smith and any clients. Written materials will include articles, blog posts, short eBooks, and any other products that can be used for the purposes of marketing a business coach's services. Written material will be delivered to clients instantaneously via secure internet connection.

"The purpose of the materials provided by Writers United is to enhance its clients' ability to market their services to their target audiences via search engine optimization, to establish their authority in the field, and to retain more clients. Research shows that males are less likely to be interested in or skilled at writing, compared to females. Coupled with the hectic schedule of a coach, there is little to no time for writing even if a male was motivated to write his own material. Writers United will provide services that bridge this gap by aggressively advertising its services through third-party freelancing websites and via business networking events where potential clients are likely to be in attendance. The primary goal of Writers United is to achieve a total gross income of $50,000 for the first year, $100,000 for year two, and $250,000 for year three.

"Many leading freelance writers charge up to $75 per hour for standard services. Writers United strives to provide affordable high quality writing by providing most services at $35 an hour, which amounts to half the cost of most writers. All material will be written by a seasoned veteran of the freelance writing industry. The startup costs for Writers United will be an estimated $20,000 for capital, $15,000 for marketing materials and $4,500 for attorney and accounting fees."

Again, it is important to save your executive summary for last; by then you will already know every important detail about your business. Besides, you can easily borrow text from your business plan to use in your summary. Now, let's forge ahead to start creating the plan itself.

Chapter 5: Your Company Description and Mission Statement

The section after the executive summary is the description and mission statement of your company, which will describe your company in great detail to your readers.

While you have some leeway and creativity in writing your company description, there are a few essential elements you must include. These will ensure that your description is specific, clear and informative.

One of the first things that you should introduce at the beginning of your description is the **name of your company**. This name should appear as it does on your business certificate. You should also note your company's **business structure**. Next, you will list the **owners** and **employees** who will be the driving factors to your company's success. Finally, you will include the **location** where you will be conducting business.

After introducing the basics of your company, you should describe the **backstory** of your company. This can include details such as when you chose to begin creating the business and why.

Your **mission statement** should follow your backstory. A mission statement is a specific declaration of your company's values and direction. Following your mission statement should be a concise explanation of your **product or service** and a description of your **target audience**. Then it is time to list your business **objectives.**

Your objectives section should contain an overview of your goals, derived from your research and data. The final item in your company description should be your **vision.** A company vision should provide a brief explanation of how you expect the company to be doing and where it will be in terms of financial success and growth a few years down the road.

Sample Company Description

Here is a fictional example of a company description for our fictional business, Writers United:

"Writers United is a new business that will provide high quality but affordable writing services to busy business coaches in the Tri-State area. Writers United is a single-member LLC operated by John Smith, former head of the freelance writing department for The Daily Press. Writers United will be operating out of Newark, New Jersey with both a physical location and remote access. **Note how this paragraph introduced the company by name, provided its pitch, named the business structure and owners and named its location of operation.**

"John Smith conceived the idea for Writers United while working as head of the freelance writing department at The Daily Press and realizing the importance of written work for the purposes of marketing a business. After noticing that many business coaches ordered custom-written articles when trying to increase their own client base, John Smith decided to address this market need by creating a small business that would specifically cater to the needs of business coaches in the area. **Note how this paragraph provides the company backstory while also providing more information about its potential clients.**

"Writers United is dedicated to making it incredibly easy for busy business coaches with little to no time and/or writing skills to access high-quality, original written content to post on their websites or otherwise use to attract customers. It also serves to connect freelance professional writers with business professionals, utilizing the benefits of internet technology. **This paragraph contains the mission statement of Writers United.**

"Writers United will provide freelance writing services that include the production of original articles, blog posts, eBooks, and any special requests for written works. The price per piece is 50 cents per word, with bulk discounts available for clients who purchase large orders. The ideal client will be a male, a business coach by profession, and a person who lacks the time and/or writing skills to produce marketable written works on his own. He also will live in New Jersey, New York, or Pennsylvania. However, the market is not limited to male clients and hopes to eventually attract female clients as well. **This paragraph includes a brief but detailed explanation on the company's service and also introduced its ideal client with a brief hint of developing its market in the future.**

"The main objectives of Writers United, for its first year of business, are: 1) to acquire $40,000 in capital for marketing, startup, and professional service costs, 2) to acquire five new clients a month via networking, online advertising, and third-party freelancing websites, 3) to achieve a $75,000 net profit during year one, through client generation and retention and by minimizing expenses, and 4) host at least four webinars per year to promote the benefits of hiring a ghostwriter to generate more clients. **This paragraph clearly states each objective for the company's first year of business.**

"Writers United's vision is to become the leading source for premium personal coaching content in the Tri-State area by providing high quality writing, exceptional customer service, and by establishing and maintaining connections with our clients."

You will note that this final paragraph ends the company description with a vision statement. This is not required, but it is commonly used as a powerful to leave the company's vision statement as the last thing on the readers' minds.

Selecting Your Name

Deciding on a business name can be the most fun and creative part of launching a new business. Sole proprietors have the option of operating under their own name. Independent contractors may choose to use their name, but many business owners create a DBA (doing business as) name. The name of your business reflects what your business is about, so you'll want to create a name that is strong, powerful and memorable. Even if you're just starting out, selecting a powerful business name can add credibility to your business and can make all the difference in your customers' first impression. So, what's in a name?

Obviously, the name of your business should reflect your products or services. It should be easy to remember and easy to spell, especially since your potential clients will want to look you up on the Internet. Business names that contain a play on words are more likely to be remembered, but it is important to ensure that your name is unique. Nobody likes an imitator; a copycat name will make your business look shady in general. It's a good idea to keep your name to a medium length. Too short of a name will likely cause problems when you go to create a domain and too long of a name may make it difficult for customers to remember how to properly spell it. It isn't a bad idea to do some test research with your potential business name before you make it official. You can ask your friends, family, and colleagues what they think about your name and you even test it in your market by utilizing message boards or networking sessions.

It's also a good idea to keep search engine optimization in mind. With search engine optimization, it's all about picking the right keywords and letting your customers come to you. For example, let's pretend you're the owner of a drug detox center in LA and you want to book as many patients as possible. A name like Coral Resorts or The Sunshine Center may sound like relaxing names for a drug detox center, but if prospective clients don't know about you yet, they won't know to type "The Sunshine Center" into Google. Instead, they're probably going to type in, "drug detox center in LA." So instead of www.thesunshinecenter.com, something like www.DrugDetoxLA.com is more likely to pop up. Therefore, it makes more economic sense to name your drug detox business Drug Detox LA.

If you're having trouble coming up with a name, it can be helpful to do a little brainstorming. Write down a list of potential keywords and start piecing together names from that list. If you get stuck, refer to a thesaurus to find alternatives. Keep in mind that you're probably going to have a company website, so it will help to check the availability of a domain name. If you don't check this early on, you could get attached to great company name, such as Bob's Burritos, only to find out that www.BobsBurritos.com is already taken.

Once you have a list of potential names, go down it and start eliminating the lesser contenders. Analyze each name from a customer's point of view. Ask yourself the pros and cons of each name. Visualize what the name reflects about your company. If you're not sure how to factor in the search engine optimization to your business name, here's a quick YouTube video that can provide a little bit more insight: How to Get on the First Page of Google by Minority Mindset.

Once you settle on the best name for your business, you will want to register it as your DBA name. This is the name that your customers will write on checks and invoices when it is time to pay you. The process for doing this varies state by state. Check with your local and state municipalities to see what steps you need to take to register your DBA name.

Selecting Your Business Structure

Not as fun as choosing a name, but equally important, is choosing your business structure. This can be a daunting and intimidating step for those who are just starting out and are confused by the different levels of business structures. Different business structures have different rules and depending on what type of business you're running, some are more appropriate than others. Some of them also have differing tax rules.

There are five main business structures to choose from:

- Sole Proprietorship – Sole proprietorships are the easiest and most straightforward business structures and are how many businesses start out. In simple terms, a sole proprietorship is one person doing business under his or her own name. You have the most control over your business in a sole proprietorship and sometimes you don't even have to formally register with your state. There are some instances where you can file your business taxes right under your own social security number. The drawbacks to having a sole proprietorship are that in the event that you are sued, your personal assets are at risk in addition to your business assets and it's also a bit more difficult for sole proprietors to obtain funding. Also, the business will cease to exist in the event of your death

- Limited Liability Company (LLC or Single-Member LLC) – LLCs are a mix between partnerships and corporations. They can have multiple owners or just one (which would be a single-member LLC); their main advantage is that the owner's personal assets are protected in the event of a legal matter. The only thing at stake is each owner's investment into the company, so it is a little easier to get funding for an LLC than a sole proprietorship. LLCs can also have managers other than the owners of the company, which is a plus for those who want to own but not work in their business. LLCs require a bit more filing and paperwork with the state, but the limited liability protection they offer are often well worth the extra work

- Partnership – Partnerships are legal structures in which two or more people come together to own a business and take responsibility for its debts. Each member of the partnership can take actions on behalf of the business. One of the biggest drawbacks is that owners are not excluded from limited liability in a partnership. It is also important for partnerships to establish contracts and make agreements on what will happen if two or more partners disagree on a business-related decision. One of the biggest advantages of a partnership is that it is taxed differently than some of the other structures. In a partnership, members do not have to pay income tax on their earnings but instead have a more complex tax requirement. Due to the complex nature of the taxing of partnerships and the fact that there are two or more people involved, forming a partnership can be expensive because much of the money will go to lawyers and accountants who can help you set it up and get it started

- Corporation – Corporations are businesses that stand as a separate entity and are run by a group of people known as directors. When you incorporate your business, company shareholders are able to trade stock within the company. A group of people are elected to serve on a board of directors; these will meet at least once a year, if not more frequently, to review the health of the company and to set its direction for the future. of the board is responsible for appointing officers to oversee the daily work at the corporate level. Shareholders of the corporation have limited liability as long as the corporation has been properly set up. Corporations pay taxes on their net income, but they are able to deduct the salaries of their shareholders. At the same time, shareholders pay taxes on their dividends, which corporations cannot deduct, leading to a double-taxation situation.

- S-Corporation – S-Corporations are like corporations, except that they are taxed using the same complex setup as a partnership. S-Corporations are smaller than regular corporations, have less than 100 shareholders within the company. They also have less stock than a regular corporation. Again, due the complex nature of its taxation, an S-Corporation can easily rack up expensive accounting fees.

For new small business, I recommend starting out as an LLC. While this may be a bit more expensive and complicated than a sole proprietorship, the personal protection it offers is worth it. Once your business begins to thrive and grow, you can then explore whether you want to form a partnership, a corporation or an S-corporation.

Selecting Your Location of Operation

There isn't much science to choosing your location. It will usually be situated in your home state and will generally be determined by the nature of your business. For most service providers, all you'll need is a small office at best, because you'll be travelling to your customers, instead of having them come to you. Whether you choose to run your business out of a home office or rent a small office space is your choice.

If you're an online freelancer and work via the computer, you can easily work from any location that has a stable internet connection. However, if you are running a business where your customers will be coming to you, then there are a few issues you'll want to keep in mind when selecting your business location.

Consider the following questions:

- "Will my customers need a place to park?"

- "Will I stand to benefit from neighboring businesses that attract more customers?"

- "Will this neighborhood attract customers or scare them away?"

- "Is my building easily accessible?"

- "How much rent can I afford?"

- "Is there enough space to conduct business at this location?"

- "Is this building zoned for commercial purposes?"

The final question is pretty important; answering it may be as simple as a quick phone call or it may require a little research, but it must be answered early on. The last thing you want to do is put a deposit down on an office space only to discover that it's not zoned for commercial operations. Some buildings are zoned for residential/commercial mixed, so it's always a good idea to check this out before signing any contracts or putting down any money.

If you choose to work from home, it's also important to check with your local and state municipalities to ensure that you're allowed to run your business out of your home. This shouldn't be much of a problem for freelancers or people who work solo, but it could be an issue if you have clients come to your home. You can usually find all the information you need on your state's homepage.

Writing Your Mission Statement

Now that you've worked your way through some of the more challenging items, it's time to have some fun again by writing your mission statement. A mission statement lets you state your business strategy in a few short sentences. If it is written carelessly and without thought, your mission statement will be nothing but empty filler. However, a solid mission statement will help you define your company's culture. A well-formulated mission statement will lay the foundation on which you can set your company's goals and objectives.

Here are a few examples of award-winning mission statements from well-known and established companies:

- **Advanced Auto Parts:** "It is the mission of Advanced Auto Parts to provide personal vehicle owners and enthusiasts with the vehicle-related products and knowledge that fulfill their wants and needs at the right price. Our friendly, knowledgeable, and professional staff will help inspire, educate, and problem-solve for our customers."

- **Southwest Airlines:** "The mission of Southwest Airlines is dedication to the highest quality of Customer Service delivered with a sense of warmth, friendliness, individual pride, and company spirit."

- **Habitat for Humanity:** "Seeking to put God's love into action, Habitat for Humanity brings people together to build homes, communities, and hope."

As you can tell from these examples, the mission statement tells the reader the specific offerings, values, and goals of a company. In the case of Advanced Auto Parts, you can tell that their target audience is people who drive and/or people who love cars. Mission statements should be short and sweet, but must be developed with careful consideration.

Here are the questions your mission statement should answer, without details, but clearly and concisely:

- What does your business stand for? For example, Google stands for organization and accessibility of information, as seen in their mission statement ("To organize the world's information and make it universally accessible and useful.")

- What are your company objectives? We will delve further into this question in the next section, but it is essential that you effectively communicate your company's objectives in this statement.

- How will you achieve your objectives? In a mission statement, you will probably communicate this using a prepositional phrase, introduced with the preposition "by." For example, if your company stood for helping the poor, the "how" statement could read, "by donating $1 for every purchase made," or "by hiring employees from poor urban areas."

- What solutions do you offer? Customers are coming to you because they have a need that you can fulfill. Don't forget to mention how you can provide your customers with a quality solution to their problems!

- Give people a sneak-peek into your company's culture. You do this by stating your company's values in your mission statement and linking it to your customers and employees. Some keywords to consider are "diversity," "equal opportunity," and "environment."

- Talk about your supplier relationships, if applicable. This is a big thing for food-related businesses. Companies often talk about where they've gotten the ingredients for their food or how the food was naturally grown and not processed, for example Consumers are increasingly interested in where you get your resources, especially in a world where health is a growing issue.

- Talk about innovation. Although the word is over-used in the business world, it's still an important concept to include in your summary. When a company shows that it values innovation, this indicates that it is striving to stand out above its competitors. It also shows a company's determination to do whatever it takes to deliver the best products or services to its customers.

It's nearly impossible to sit down and bang out the perfect mission statement on your first try, so I recommend putting aside some extra time to work on yours. Many people find it easier to begin writing without a word count limitation and then edit it down until all of the most important information is contained within 30 to 100 words.

Don't be afraid to use colorful words; experiment with different word choices and don't feel that you have to rush to the finish line! Take as much time as you need. Step away for a day and then return to it with fresh perspective. Brainstorm, brainstorm, brainstorm and don't stop until you've created the absolute perfect sentence or two that ultimately describes your company. Enlist a friend, family member, or another business owner to read your mission statement and give you feedback. Ask questions and probe your reviewers to get down to their gut responses to your specific word choices as well as the overall meaning.

Defining Your Objectives

In a business, objectives are realities you want to experience within your company and goals define the actions you take to get there. For example, if your objective is for your products to become the leading brand of dental care, your goal might be to sell 1 million tubes of toothpaste, 2 million toothbrushes, and 3 million containers of dental floss by January of the next year. Setting up objectives and establishing their supportive goals is crucial if you want to grow and succeed as a business. When you want to achieve a specific outcome, a goal is your number one resource to help you get there.

When it comes to running a business, your objectives will change as you work to keep winning and retaining customers. For example, the objective for an LLC company may be to ultimately incorporate. From that point, a fresh objective could be established to hire 100 employees, next to establish multiple locations, and so on. Objectives are important for keeping your customer base happy. Common customer-oriented objectives often include enhancing your customer service or developing more attractive products and services. As you can imagine, setting goals and objectives at the business level can be overwhelming in its complexity, so it is important to approach them with the best goal-setting strategies possible.

It can be helpful to establish your mission statement prior to writing out your goals. This will provide at least an idea of your business direction in terms of ethics, values and of course, success. Once you've narrowed your objectives down in support of your mission statement, you can begin to separate each one into component parts and organize goals you must reach to ultimately achieve the objective.

While your mission statement is limited in size, objective definition and goal-setting are wordy propositions. When writing out your objectives and their attendant goals, there is no word limit. In fact, you should be as detailed and precise as possible.

Once you have written out your objectives, you can identify which ones qualify as long-term objectives and begin breaking these down into smaller and more manageable goals. Don't forget to give each goal a due date so you have a sense of accountability and a clear time frame in which to complete it. It's also a good idea to hold a regular review of your progress toward your goals, so that they stay fresh in your mind. Periodic review also helps you notice your progress, which can be a tremendous motivator.

Setting goals can easily spiral into an uncontrollable mess, even if your intentions are good. I've experienced this myself. For many people, goal-setting is exciting. Vigorously motivated people can often come up with a list of 50 goals. Of course, it's unrealistic to try and achieve 50 different goals at once so prioritization and ordering goals in sequence is the best way to tame the whole herd. I recommend limiting your current pursuit to between three and five goals at one time. Once you've successfully reached the goals on your list, you can move on to the next goals in sequence, thus making progress toward the accomplishment of your objectives.

It can be helpful to break your business objectives into categories to allow you to prioritize each one. For example, you may have business-focused objectives, customer-focused objectives, employee-focused objectives and creativity objectives. Once you've categorized all of your objectives, you can then determine which goals are more important to tackle first in support of those objectives. For example, if your employee-focused objective is to improve working conditions, it may be a good idea to make some progress toward that objective before you tackle the objective of releasing five new products; happier employees generally lead to more effective production. Of course, if your employees are already thriving and happy, it would make more sense to begin focusing on your customers. Overall, it comes down to a sense of balance.

Finally, it's important to separate short-term objectives from your long-term objectives. Short-term objectives can easily be reached in a few days, weeks, or months. However it may take years to complete a long-term objective. Sometimes it's easier to break down a long-term objective into a sequence of short-term goals.

It's a really great idea to write out your goals somewhere. There are numerous benefits to writing down your goals, whether they are personal or business-related. Some people prefer to handwrite their goals and track them in a notebook but there are also some great computer programs that can help you.

One of my favorite tools is Microsoft OneNote. It is basically an online notebook where you can keep all of your notes and ideas. You can dedicate a single notebook to keeping track of your goals, allowing you to monitor your progress toward each goal, manage related to-do lists, and store notes and tips. OneNote allows you to easily store all of your notes digitally. You can include multiple different media there, including pictures. While one benefit of handwriting your goals is that you're more likely to remember them, handwritten notes can easily be lost. My best recommendation is to handwrite your goals to burn them into your head, then take a picture and transfer them into OneNote. That way, you'll the memory-saving benefit of writing them down, plus you'll never need to worry about losing or misplacing the information. Even if you don't use OneNote, you can still take a picture of your handwritten notes and transfer the picture into your word processor.

Don't be afraid to solicit your employees' input on goals. While many companies set goals from a corporate level, there are also many companies – both large and small –that let employees in on the process. It may be easier to get your employees' input in a small business, but I also know of large companies that have successfully included all of their employees in the process. If you've ever worked in an organization that values the opinions of its employees, you know that sometimes the best ideas come from the people who are working in the field.

Overall, any kind of goal should follow the principles outlined by the acronym, S.M.A.R.T.:

- Specific – Is your goal specific and clear? Does it answer the "Who, What, When, Where, Why and How" questions?

- Measurable – Can you quantify your end result? If you're selling something, how much do you need to sell? If you're recruiting, how many people do you need to attract? You will never know when you've reached your goal unless you give it a clear ending point. That ending point is only clear when it can be measured.

- Attainable – Provided that everyone involved works together, are your goals reachable? Do they reflect the skill sets of the people who will be doing the work?

- Realistic – Are your goals realistic? Do you have enough resources to carry you to the endpoint?

- Timely – Is the given time frame for achieving your goals appropriate? Do your goals have a due date?

I recommend checking each of your business goals against the S.M.A.R.T. criteria to ensure that they all hold. If a goal definition doesn't answer every question, it should be either redefined to match the criteria or scrapped outright.

Writing Your Company Vision

Your company vision differs from its mission in that a vision is what you see as the end purpose of your company. When you have a vision it gives you a guideline for developing your business and helps you determine how you want it to impact your customers, the world, your community, etc. For example, Bill Gates envisioned a world in which everyone would a computer in their home. That was the vision behind the launching of Microsoft Corporation. It is important to know that your company's vision is not directly correlated to your company's success – it's just a simple guide to the direction you want your company to go. However, your vision can help you figure out which actions can help to make your dream come true.

Have you ever been on a job interview when your prospective employer asked you, "Where do you see yourself in five years?" By asking yourself that simple question of your business, you can be on your way to developing your own company vision. My recommendation is to grab a piece of paper or open a blank word document and write this statement: "In X years, I envision my company as _____". By filling in these blanks, you are on the road to creating your company vision. Your vision doesn't have to be long. In fact, it can be very general. However, by writing out your vision statement, you then also have a visual aid that will you set your objectives.

Chapter 6: Describing Your Product or Service

In this section of your business plan, you will have the opportunity to provide your readers with an in-depth description of your company's products and services. The most important opportunity you have in this section is to show your audience how your product or service stands out from its competition. The length of this section will depend on the kind of products and services you will be providing. For example, a business that has created its own product line will have a longer product description than a business that sells existing products at discount prices.

Other important details to include in this section are dates when your products will be available, how you have arranged your pricing and who are your suppliers, if applicable. If you have applied for or already have any trademarks, copyrights or other legal claims on your products or services, you should include them in this section.

What to Include in Your Descriptions

Physical Attributes – You want to physically describe your product or service. Include information on colors, sizes, materials, textures, and fragrances, as applicable. For a service, you can describe what the customer can expect to receive.

Be as specific as possible. For example, a good product description would be as follows: "The child's beanbag chair comes in hot pink or bright blue, it measures 24 inches in height and 36 inches in width, and is made of genuine leather with a filling of memory-foam beads. Each chair will be priced to the customer at $49.99." To describe an article-writing service, you could say, "The article-writing package includes three 500-word articles on any topic written in Open Office and delivered via email within five business days of ordering. This package will cost the customer $100."

Special Aspects – In this subsection, you can describe any special aspects of your product or service that make it unique. This allows you to provide in-depth details that may not be immediately evident in the description. It also can highlight specifics that make your offering superior to anything similar on the market. For example, the beanbag chair described above has five small Velcro-closeable pockets along the sides that can hold snacks, small toys, etc. Each pocket measures four square inches. The bag can also be folded up for easy storage. For the service offering above, the article-writing package includes up to two revisions and a commercial license.

The best way to fill out this section is to pretend like you're describing an actual picture of your product. Include the slightest detail, no matter how minor it may appear.

How the Product Can Improve Customers' Lives – In this subsection, you will describe the positive impact your product or service will have on the lives of your target audience. For example, the child's beanbag chair, with its several compartments and easy storage, will make it easier for parents to keep their children's favorite belongings together when they sit and watch television and simplifies the storage process. The article-writing package will make it easier for hard-working business coaches to access online marketing material and using the time they would take to write it themselves to interact with their most important clients. It is important to include every benefit your target audience will receive when they purchase your product or service; you don't know which benefit will touch the heart of a reader.

What makes it Unique – In the final subsection, you will describe how and why your product or service is different from similar offerings from your competitors. This can be a challenge, especially if multiple similar products are available in the marketplace. You'll need to review each competing product, looking for weaknesses or gaps in service that you plan to address through your product.

One popular way to set yourself apart from the crowd is to advertise that you're selling a metaphor rather than an actual product or service. For example, a fast-food restaurant might be selling you "convenience" disguised as burgers and fries; a cosmetics company might be selling you "beauty" rather than moisturizer and face cream. These metaphors can also put you ahead of the game when it comes to winning hearts and minds of potential customers.

If you're selling a product or service at competitive price points, or using a nontraditional sales outlet, this point will also be important to note. If the pricing will be vary across different outlets (for example, online pricing vs. in-store pricing), you will want to point this out in your description.

This is also a strategic place to communicate key results you uncovered as part of your market research. Always include customer demographics and trending statistics. Help your readers look at your product or service from your customers' point of view. This will reveal what they *really* want and will display the underlying subconscious motivations behind your product's attractiveness.

Fulfilment – In this subsection, you will explain how the orders for your product or service will be fulfilled. For example, a grocery store may receive a variety of items from different suppliers. Milk may come from one supplier, produce from another, meat from a third, and so on. In this case, the store would purchase from each vendor, anticipating what its customers will buy.

An author who sells his books through a third-party publishing website may have the on-demand publishing company as his supplier, where he can order a certain number of hard copies to sell. He may also advertise his books through the publisher, where readers can order at their leisure. The suppliers of a freelance writing service could be the writers who own the company themselves.

It is important to know who will be supplying, or helping you supply, your product or service. If you're selling something, it's essential that you make your offering as easy to access as possible. Your backers want the assurance that your pipeline to the market is clearly defined; they want it as clean and straightforward as possible.

Tools Needed – What tools or technology will you need in order to produce or manufacture your product or service? Here is where you will list things such as computer programs, robotic technology, materials or resources that will be required to create your product or service and pass it on to your customers. For each item, provide a brief description of the part it will play in the production process.

Future Recommendations – If you take a few moments to think about it, you will realize that certain products may sell great at one period in time and then not sell at all a few years later. This has been the case with the transition from records to cassettes to CDs to mp3s and VHS tapes to DVDs to online streaming services. You have likely seen how cellular phone technology has changed from the early 80's to now. You can even see this online, with the phasing out of once-popular social media websites like Friendster and MySpace, which were quickly dominated by platforms such as Facebook and Instagram. Even though it may be hard to visualize right now, those social media platforms stand a chance of being dominated by something even bigger.

Companies that understand the concept of trends and are able to position themselves ahead of the change. I once worked with a client who had a booming business in the days of dial-up internet connections. The business failed when the next big change in internet came along.

To prevent this from happening to you, it is imperative that you and your team remain alert to trends in the world. Let your company learn to ride the waves of change and be the first to offer the next big thing

When it comes to writing out the description of your product or service, it's helpful to format it in an easy-to-read manner, especially if you're going to be putting those descriptions online. Leave out technical jargon that your customer may not understand and point out the benefits in glowing terms, so that your customer will be persuaded to buy. Bullet points are wonderful for this purpose; they allow you to list details succinctly in short, keyword-laden phrases that pack a punch.

Bullet points also create welcome white space. Too much text with no breaks in between can be hard to absorb, especially on a screen. Short clumps of information help your brain group similar facts together and better remember them.

You may find it beneficial to work with an experienced copywriter to help you create your descriptions. Copywriters often have an extensive knowledge on how to write persuasive, sharp content that can boost your sales and drive customer traffic toward your product.

Chapter 7: Industry and Market Analysis

An industry analysis is the part of your business plan that portrays measureable information, backed up by the numbers and documented research reports, to describe your target market. The purpose is to explain buying trends and show why your business will be at an advantage within that market.

Not only is your industry analysis important for showing everything you can about your potential target audience, it is a valuable tool for convincing investors to sink money in your business venture. If your industry analysis does not demonstrate how your business will address a need within a certain demographic, why would anybody invest their money in it? They'd be supporting an almost guaranteed flop! On the other hand, writing a great industry analysis on your first try can smooth the road for reaching investors and ultimately customers, while charting a course toward business success.

This document should be no more than three pages long. these sections will be described in greater detail later, but for now, here is what you'll want to include in your industry analysis

- Industry Outlook Overview. This snapshot should give your readers the important aspects of the industry in brief form. Describe the players in this industry, noting how many are major players, but not overlooking minor players and those that are growing swiftly. Include a brief description of the development of the industry and the key drivers behind its growth. This naturally leads to a summary of future growth predictions.

- Challenges. Briefly describe both current and anticipated challenges to both the industry itself and the ability of your business to enter and perform profitably within it. This would include government regulations, lack of funds or expertise, etc.

- A market analysis (described below)

- Analysis of customers.

- Your projections of how your business will successfully navigate the waters within this industry.

Market Analysis

A market analysis portrays your target market – the customers who will be buying your products or services. It will help to ensure that you are marketing your products or services correctly, targeting the right groups of people with your message. I will walk you through the details of creating a market analysis a little later. For now, however, here is what will be included:

- A description of your industry.

- A description of your target market.

- An analysis of your competition.

- Projected growth of your business.

- How you plan to comply with any industry constraints or regulations.

Writing an Industry Outlook Overview

An industry outlook is a snapshot of the industry within which your business operates. An industry outlook shows where your industry is positioned within its life cycle, whether it's rapidly growing with many competing rivals or it has stagnated, presenting few opportunities for fresh growth. Writing an industry outlook for your business is important because investors are not going to want to invest in a business in an industry that is dying or that cannot progress. One purpose of including an industry outlook in your market analysis is so you can convince potential investors and anyone else involved in your business that their contributions will be worthwhile.

A well-written industry outlook should include information on where your industry currently is, any trends within it, information on your competitors including a list of their strengths and weaknesses and any obstacles that may stand in the way of your business getting into the market. You must also demonstrate the value of your business within the industry and how you will stand out from your competitors. All of this information should be supported with factual market research. You should then analyze the industry as a whole and then show where your business would fit into it. For example, if your business is going to serve your entire county, include an international-level industry analysis and then reduce it to cover your country, state, and county. If your business is only going to serve a local community, you'll want to include the level of your hometown.

If you're not sure where to begin when writing your industry outlook overview, you can begin by researching answers to the following questions, as they pertaining to your business and the industry:

- How much money does the entire industry make annually? What is it slated to make this year? What did it make last year?

- How many products or services does the entire industry sell annually? How many is it currently slated to sell this year? How about last year?

- What are the current sales trends in your industry?

- Who are your main competitors? What special and unique services do they offer as part of their marketing strategy?

- Are there any obstacles that will prevent or make it difficult for your business to break into the industry?

- How does technology affect your industry, if at all?

- How will you primarily market your products or services? How does that differ from your competition?

- Does your industry have to adhere to government regulations, such as OSHA or Fair Trade regulations? Will it be affected by the environment? The current economic state?

- How do customer buying trends affect your industry, if at all?

By answering these questions, you can begin to put the answers together to form several short paragraphs that describe the general overview of your industry. While these paragraphs shouldn't be painfully detailed, they should be specific, clear and get right to the point about the current state of the industry. You can save the details for later parts of the industry outlook.

How to Perform Market Research

The purpose of market research is to provide new businesses with information on the wants and needs of their target market. They can then use this information when developing their products or services so they know that their target market will be more likely to buy from them and not their competitors. Existing businesses can use market research to determine if their current customers are happy with their products or services.

Identifying and Introducing Your Target Market

Your target audience is the group of people toward whom you will be marketing your products or services. Remember your unique selling proposition from the last chapter? That proposition must be relevant to your target audience. For example, you wouldn't sell the idea of convenience to children but you *would* probably be selling it to the busy single mom or dad who cares for those children. Your target audience must be specific and well-researched; otherwise you will probably miss out on key sales opportunities. Sometimes businesses will completely revamp and restructure their target audience in the middle of operations. That's what Kellogg did when its sales began to decline. While many businesses big and small find it necessary to change their target audience years down the road, it can be a pain to have to go back and make a bunch of changes. That's why it's important to try and get it right the first time. In this chapter, you will discover the best ways to identify the best target audience for your business.

Your target audience is the group of consumers to whom you will market your products and services. The purpose of having a target audience is so you know who you will be marketing too and how you will go about doing so. Take for example the freelance writer who is looking to take on new clients, who happen to be business coaches with little to no time or skills to write. He or she may post an article of his or her website entitled "The benefits of hiring a ghostwriter for busy business coaches," or "How business coaches can boost their client base without having to clear their busy schedule." As you can see from the example, the article specifically calls upon busy business coaches and then entices them to see how the freelance writer's services can help them.

In the above example, the freelance writer knows who his or her audience is but many startups have trouble defining their audience at first. Without properly defining your audience, your marketing efforts will be pointless. One good way to start is to develop a demographic picture of what your ideal client looks like. A demographic picture often includes gender, marital status, age, occupation, residence and income.

For example, your ideal client may look like:

- A married man in his 40s that is an entrepreneur who lives in Chicago and makes over $75,000 per year

- A child between the ages of 5 and 7 who live with a single parent in NYC that makes less than $50,000 per year

- A newly-wedded couple in their 30s who currently rent in urban areas of New Jersey whose median income is $65,000 per year

There is no limitation to what your ideal client looks like. Yours will be unique based on what you're selling, what area you're selling in and to whom your products or services will appeal. Although having an ideal client picture may seem like the answer to all of your marketing needs, it only scratches the surface. Once you have it figured out, you'll then need to go even deeper and determine what problem your ideal client has that you can help them solve. Existing businesses can look at their previous clients to find a pattern of buying motivation but startups will have to utilize guessing power at first. Once you know what will motivate your customers to buy from you, you can then use that knowledge to position your marketing strategies.

How to Define Your Target Audience

Many startups make the mistake of thinking that their audience is everyone all over the world who wants to buy their product or service. However, that definition of a target audience is way too broad and generalized. Some startups already have a good idea of who their product or service is meant for but sometimes the answer isn't always clear. However, there are some steps you can take to easily figure it out.

First, you can perform an analysis of your product or service. Make a list of everything that your product or service has to offer someone and then brainstorm how that could benefit somebody. Once you have your list of benefits, you can begin to create your ideal client picture. Again, we can use the example of the freelance writer to highlight this point. The freelance writer offers high-quality writing. A benefit of high-quality writing is that it will likely come off as professional. You can then make a list of **who** can benefit from high-quality writing that will make their services look professional. As you know, this fictional freelance writer targets business coaches but you could also think of doctors, lawyers, accountants, life coaches, marketers, dentists or anyone along those lines. Next, put yourself in their customers' shoes. If you were looking for a business coach, wouldn't you want to know that you're spending your money on somebody really great and professional? Who would you be most likely to pick – the one who has a blog on their website full of knowledgeable information or the one who has nothing more than a landing page with their contact info? Therefore, professional writing is more likely to attract more clients to that business coach.

Once you have finished your brainstorming and picked out **who** can benefit from your product or service, you can then begin to narrow things down even more. Again, this is where you can begin to fill in the blanks with gender, marital status, age, occupation, residence and income. Of course, you're not limited to those categories. You can also consider factors such as race, religion, level of education, family size, hobbies, etc. The types of factors you can use are endless. Again, if you're not sure how to fit your ideal client into each factor, you can use the brainstorming method to see which details fit best. Once you have filled in all of the specifics, you can even go so far as to use psychology to jumpstart your ideal clients' motivation to buy. Psychological factors such as control, family values, discovery, humor, self-expression, self-improvement, self-esteem, timesaving and even romance can strongly influence whether a customer decides to buy something.

As you wrap up the process of identifying your ideal client, there a few more key questions to ask yourself to ensure that you've picked the right audience. First and most importantly, you'll want to make sure that your audience can afford to buy your product or service. Otherwise, what's the point of marketing to a group who cannot even afford to pay you? You'll also want to make sure that your audience is large enough. Sometimes getting *too* specific can leave you with a very small group of people to work with, therefore leaving you with a limited earning potential. If you find that your audience turns out to be too small, you can go back and see if there are multiple small niches that can benefit from your business, expanding your earning potential.

Competition

Next, you will need to describe your competition. This section should generally include a description of your major competitors, how their services and products are unique and how your business stands out from them. I don't want to go into too much detail on competition right now, as I have dedicated an entire chapter on it. You can leave this section blank for now and then go back to it and fill it in after reading Chapter 3.

Regulations

In this section, you have the opportunity to analyze any kinds of government regulations to which your business must adhere. This will require some more research on your part, as different industries and different types of business will have to adhere to different regulations. For example, a sole proprietor freelance writer who gets paid by the job and who pays himself will not have to worry about payment regulations and standards, such as minimum wage, minimum working age requirements or overtime hours. However, an entrepreneur who wants to own a set of fast-food restaurants will need to think about labor law. While the entrepreneur does not have to worry about the taxation of alcohol and cigarettes, the proprietor of a convenience store will and so on.

Some factors to think about in this section include:

- Labor Law

- Occupational Health and Safety

- Compensation/Payment Laws

- Food Safety Regulations

- Unions

- Liquor Licensing/Cigarette Sales

- Taxation

- Wastage Disposal

- General Business Ethics

By doing industry research, you can easily find out what kinds of government regulations you will need to adhere to in your business but the above are just a few of the most common. You can then explain how your business plans to work the regulations into its operations.

Sample Industry Outlook

Here, you'll find a sample of an industry outlook that you can use to model your own. For the purposes of this example, I've just included completely fictional research but the way it is written should give you the idea on how to go about it. This example will be an industry outlook for the fictional freelance writing business.

The Freelance Writing Industry

According to the Freelance Writer's Union, the freelance writing industry generates $1.5 billion in revenue every year. For 2017, it is estimated that the industry will pull in an additional $500,000. The total amount of revenue last year was $1.3 billion. According to the same organization, the best-selling writing service was article ghostwriting followed by blog-writing followed by novel ghostwriting. An estimated 20 million articles were written by freelance writers for their clients in 2016.

The BLS shows that professional servants such as doctors, lawyers, accountants and coaches spent $2 billion on marketing services in 2016, broken down as follows:

- $200,000 on mass media advertising

- $300,000 on social media marketing

- $250,000 on website content

- $250,000 on blogs and guest blogs

- $500,000 on ghostwriting books

- $500,000 on content-specific articles

These growing figures suggest that there is a high market demand for freelance writers to provide original content for these professionals to provide as their own material. Jake Smith, director of marketing for LoveYourLife, a corporate-owned life-coaching franchise said in 2016 interview, "Professionals who provide specialty services such as accounting are getting busier and busier and have no time or specialized skills to generate valuable written content on their own. However, they know that written content is the key to generating more clients." Because these professionals rely on their clients as their sole source of revenue, there is a growing demand for more clients.

Writers United in the Freelance Writing Industry

In New Jersey, Pennsylvania and New York alone, where the total average income is $175,000 annually, there are 50,000 business coaches, making it an ideal market for a freelance writing-based service such as Writers United. High-quality and in-demand business coaches want to continue building their client base and are willing to pay top dollar for the best content. Market research reveals that 9 out of 10 business coaches surveyed in the Tri-State area would prefer to hire a third-party freelance writer to research and write original content for them to post on their websites to attract clients and 8 out of 10 said they would prefer to pay more for a guarantee of better quality and faster delivery.

Competition of Writers United

There are currently 100 freelance writers who advertise their services in the Tri-State area. However, less than 75% promise high-quality and none of them mention anywhere in their advertisements that they will deliver at the speed of lightning. The majorities of these businesses have only started within the last 3 years and have yet to leave their mark in the area. The market is currently open to a leader.

Writers United is unique because instead of just selling freelance writing services, it focuses on selling high-quality and speed. Our slogan is "High-Quality Writing at The Speed of Light." We also aim to treat each individual client as if we have serviced them for years, giving them the feeling of being our only client. We will cater to their every demand. We will also be offering bulk freelance-writing content packages for a discounted price, a strategy that no other writer in the area currently offers.

Chapter 8: Defining Your Company's Operations

You will use this section of your business plan to define and describe your company's operations. Operations refers to your business locations, supplies, labor, and the methods you use to conduct business internally to ultimately provide your customers with top-quality products and services. The details that you include in this section will differ depending on the nature of your business, so we will go over everything that you may need to know.

The purpose of this section for new businesses is to describe your plans for each part of your operations. Very small businesses or those in a single-member LLC may not think that operations planning may be necessary but that idea couldn't be further from the truth. Your business may start out small but imagine what happens if it quickly begins to successfully grow. A one or two person business working out of a basement may suddenly find it difficult to manage everything correctly, leading to the possibility of losing valuable customers. When you have a plan for your business' operations in place, you can sleep soundly at night knowing that you will not have to worry about your small operations collapsing under pressure when the need for a bigger operations comes around.

The best way to begin this section of your plan is to list anything you've already accomplished in terms of your operations. For startup businesses, this could mean having already rented out your office space or already having hired a management team. Again, this section will be unique based on your situation. For some startups, there may not be anything to list.

Next, you begin the operations planning process. This section should include details on how you plan to conduct operations once your business gets up and running. You should include details on your production process, the anticipated location of operations, general operation information, industry-related affiliations, labor requirements, information on your suppliers, and information on your quality control processes and standards. Let's take a look at each of these topics a little more closely.

Production Process

Your production process outlines how you intend to produce the product or service you are selling. It includes your contingency plan for obstacles that may arise during production. If the production may pose a safety hazard to your customers or any employees involved in its production, it is important to disclose that information here. You will also describe the processes you are establishing to keep those hazards to a minimum.

This section should include details on the kind of equipment and materials you'll need for production, including how much they will cost. You will note how long the production process will take for each order and outline your plan for managing backorders and high-demand orders. This is the best place to include any testing results you may have amassed, such as customer acceptance or price-testing.

Here you will also include how you intend to get your products to your customers, whether via retail store or shipping services. Finally, you should include information on the cost of each product or service as well as note how you plan to store and keep track of inventory.

Sample Production Process

Let's take a look at an example of a production process outline for a cupcake business:

The production of cupcakes will require:

- Two stainless steel ovens with 10 baking racks ($1,000 each)

- 20 baking sheets (10 for each oven) ($50 each)

- 5 oversized galvanized mixing bowls ($50 each)

- 5 high-speed automatic mixers ($100 each)

- 2 sets of heat-proof oven mitts ($75 each)

- One large refrigerator for cooling ($700)

Materials for each batch of 12 cupcakes will require:

- 20 pounds of flour ($100)

- 10 pounds of sugar ($50)

- 15 pounds of baking powder ($45)

- One tub of buttercream icing ($50)

- One tub of multi-colored sprinkles ($50)

- One tub of walnuts ($50)

All employees will be required to wear heatproof oven mitts when handling the production of cupcakes to prevent burns and other heat-related injuries. We will also post several food allergy disclaimers in our stores, menus and online website to inform customers of the presence of nuts in our cupcakes. Each batch of 12 cupcakes takes 2 hours to make including preparation and decorating. Our one dozen counts of cupcakes will be priced at $9.99, which is 30% lower than our competitor, The Doughnut Shop, and can be achieved by buying all ingredients in bulk from our suppliers. All cupcakes will be available for sale in our two storefronts. We will perform an inventory of our ingredients as well as equipment once every quarter.

Location of Operation and General Operations

This section should include information about where your business will be located and its hours of operation. Here, you will include a description of what your building or office space looks like and include copies of any rental agreements or mortgage terms. Note whether your landlord or your company is in charge of real-estate-related issues, such as property tax payment and renters' insurance. State the square footage of your space and include pictures and layouts if you can.

If there are any challenges to your location, such as limited parking space or existing next to an active volcano, you'll want to note those facts and explain how you plan to make it easier for customers to access your location. If you are open to the public, you can list your hours of operation and your physical address in this section as well. For the cupcake business, this section would likely look like this:

Our business will have two storefronts and one baking facility. The storefronts will be located in downtown Newark at 555 Ferry Street and one on the Atlantic City boardwalk at 123 Boardwalk Way. Both retail spaces are 500 sq. feet and rented on a yearly lease that renews in October of each year at $5,000 per month. See Appendix A and B for pictures of each storefront and parking area.

Our location in Newark has 30 parking spaces, three of which are handicap accessible. The lot can receive traffic from the north and west sides. Our Atlantic City location will rely solely upon the foot traffic brought in by other businesses in the area as well as by the beachfront.

Our baking facility, illustrated in Appendix C, is located in Jersey City and is rented on a yearly basis that renews in November at $10,000 per month. The landlords at all 3 locations are responsible for the payments of property taxes and leave no responsibility to our company.

The hours of operation will be the same for each storefront as follows:

Monday: 9am-5pm
Tuesday: 9am-5pm
Wednesday: 9am-5pm
Thursday: 9am-5pm
Friday: 9am-5pm
Saturday: 9am-8pm
Sunday: 7am-4pm

If you have chosen a remote-based business or a business that is completely conducted online, you should explain the advantages of not needing a physical location.

Industry-Related Affiliations

In this section, you can list any industry-related affiliations that you already have, such as memberships to organizations. The main purpose of listing these affiliations is to demonstrate to your reader that you're connected to the industry and to assure others that you are aware of any government-imposed regulations to which your business will need to adhere.

Labor Requirements

In this section, you will include details of your hiring process and the amount and type of support you plan to hire. This is a good place to include a brief top-down description of your management structure. For example, a large retail management system might look something like this:

- President -> Vice President -> CEO -> Regional Manager -> District Manager -> Store Manager -> Shift Supervisor -> Cashier

Your management system breakdown will depend on the nature and size of your business but as you can see from the example above, it will include everyone, from the highest position all the way down to the lowest job. A company with a breakdown as shown above will probably need fewer district managers and store managers but more cashiers to run their operation.

Here, you will list how many positions you will have and how many you need yet to fill. You can include terms of employment, starting wages, required hours, and anything else that pertains to your hiring process.

You will also include your hiring goals. For example, your goal may be to hire 100 managers and 10 cashiers by the end of the first quarter. Here, you can also include your plan for recruitment and your detail the hiring process. For example, will your business require paper applications or will all applicants have to apply online? Who in your business will be in charge of reviewing applications and scheduling applicants for interviews? Will you require a drug screening and/or background checks? These are a couple of important questions to ask yourself of your hiring plan.

Information on Suppliers

In this section, you will introduce your established as well as needed suppliers and vendors and lay out how much money you will be putting out for supplies and equipment. Include any terms and conditions already agreed upon. For existing vendors, note how often they will be coming to your location and what services they will be providing.

For example, which company is providing the licensed soft drinks in your beverage cooler and how many times per week will they be coming in to restock them? This section is also a good place to include a contingency plan in the event that you will need to change suppliers or if your supplier can no longer provide you with the materials that you need in order to conduct your business.

Information on Quality Control

In this section, you will include your quality control processes showing how you plan to deliver high-quality and top-rated products and services to your consumers. Include any quality management processes and standards that your employees must follow. For example, the business owner may be responsible for accepting or rejecting material from suppliers based on its quality. If your company advertises "the finest cupcakes in New Jersey" and your supplier is providing you with less than quality materials, then you will not be able to live up to your claims. Your accountant must also be able to meet tight and important deadlines for paying your company's estimated taxes on a quarterly basis. Your cashiers must be friendly and willing to help all customers. It's a good idea to ensure that all aspects of your business have quality control processes in place. Otherwise, it can affect the overall quality of your business.

Customer service strategies are a huge part of your quality control strategy. After all, what's worse than an angry and upset customer? One of my wisest bosses once told me that if a customer has a bad experience, they're three times as likely to tell their friends and family about it than if they had a good experience.

The best businesses usually benefit from positive word-of-mouth statements anyway, especially if customers are shocked at the greatness of the company. However, the statement about customers telling everyone about bad experiences is unfortunately true as well. When I worked in retail, it was amazing how often a single angry customer would call the corporate office, post their upsetting experience on the company's social media pages and plaster a bad review on every imaginable review website. In contrast, the customers who wanted to share a great experience, usually only used one or two reporting options.

When it comes to implementing great customer service quality standards, here are a few important questions to ask:

- What standards and expectations will you communicate to your customers about customer service? For example, will every cashier smile and say thank you or the customer gets free service? Will your business stand behind the products its selling 100% or you'll refund your customer's money?

- How will your customers communicate with your business in regards to questions, comments and complaints? How will your company handle each inquiry?

- How will you provide quick and efficient customer service?

- How does your customer service program differ from that of your competition?

Operations Conclusion

Once you reach the end of writing your operations section, the best way to determine if you've done it correctly is to ask yourself a few questions of your content:

- Can the reader identify my target audience and products or services?

- Can the reader identify all important information on our location?

- Can the reader identify what equipment, resources and materials our business will require?

- Can the reader fully understand our production process?

- Can the reader identify our suppliers and vendors and fully understand our purchasing process?

- Can the reader easily identify how we will manage and conduct our inventories?

- Can the reader easily identify our quality control measures for each aspect of our business?

Chapter 9: Building and Describing Your Management Team

You may be wondering why you need to include information on your management team in your business plan if the driving factor behind your business is your product or service. However, your product or service is only part of the driving factor behind your business' success! Your management team is just as important. In fact, the quality of your management team can actually influence whether or not a potential investors decides to back your business. Providing an accurate reflection of your management team in your business plan also enables you to better manage your team.

This section should include the breakdown of your management structure, if applicable. The purpose of including a breakdown of your management structure is to show potential investors that there is a clear line of communication between the top of your organization to its lowest level. All in all, this section should include information on your business structure and management breakdown as well as include information on your management team and any other important information related to your management team. Its length and complexity will depend on the size and scope of your business.

Management Breakdown

First and most important, you should restate what business structure you are using. A quick review of the most common business structures are sole proprietorships, LLCs or single-member LLCs, partnerships, corporations and s-corporations. If you are using a more complex structure, such as a partnership or corporation, this is the best section to elaborate on its details. Explain who has stake in the structure, what percentage each stakeholder owns, etc. If there is also a chain of command throughout your business, it is important to include that here as well. Think back to the example in the previous chapter showing the hypothetical management system breakdown from the top of the chain (President) to the very bottom (Cashier).

Recruiting Your Team

Initially, you may be tempted to be the only person wearing multiple hats, so to speak. You may think that you can oversee your entire business by yourself by being the only person who performs a service or who builds a product while heading your marketing efforts and staying on top of your accounting. While it is possible (but certainly not easy) for some sole proprietors to do that, it doesn't set you up for a very high chance of having a successful business. I've seen some business owners do that and things did not work out very well for them. It started off all easy and fine until they discovered that they couldn't handle everything by themselves and then began to feel overwhelmed. Even small businesses will need multiple managers and/or employees to take some of the pressure off on the owners, mainly so that they can own, not be, their business.

Many people believe they can easily turn their passion into a money-making success but if it's only them working the business, it's highly likely that they will quickly fall out of love with their passion or talent and shut down. Smart business owners who do not attempt to do it all often do not lose their passion or talent and often go on to be more successful. By hiring the right management team, you can be a smart business owner.

How To Form A Management Team

My first piece of advice is to focus on hiring people with the right set of skills for the respective job positions that you need. It's common for the friends and family of business owners to often ask, "Can I have a job?" and it's not always easy to say no to somebody who is close to you. Of course, it depends on what skillsets a person needs for different types of job. If you own a restaurant and your brother asks you if your 18 year old nephew can have a job as a busboy, then it may make sense to give him a chance, because those types of jobs are perfect for younger kids with limited experience. Of course, if you owned a security company and your brother asked you to hire your 18 year old unexperienced nephew with no technology background for a programming job, it would not make sense to take him on.

Where To Find Recruits

Again, your recruiting strategy will depend on the size and scope of your business. Businesses that need entry-level employees, such as fast food cashiers or shift managers, most likely have a good chance of finding some great prospective candidates on job search websites such as Craigslist or Monster.com. If you're looking for someone to lead your marketing department, you can still have some luck on job search websites but I think you're better off looking on more professional platforms, such as LinkedIn, where you can see your prospective candidate's credentials, educational background, accomplishments, professional recommendations and more. There are also private businesses that can help you with your candidate search for a fee but in return, they often find great, pre-qualified candidates that are likely to be great fits to the position. Additionally, you can utilize networking to find prospective candidates. Targeted networking – for example, looking for a graphic designer at a Graphic Designers Convention – is the way to go.

Manager Profiles

The profiles section of your business plan is very simple to write, as you will just need to provide the profiles of each member of your team in the different areas of your business. For example, you can provide a set of profiles for your sales team and a different set for your marketing team. The types of categories and numbers of profiles you choose to include will depend on the size and nature of your business. Your personal profile should come before the profiles of your key managers because your readers will want to know more information on who is behind the business. While startups will probably not have to worry about having a huge management team from the start, it's always acceptance to include the top 5 or so most important profiles if you have a very large team. To ensure that you include all of the most important information, you can make sure you've included everything on this checklist, including in your personal profile:

- The employee's role or function

- A brief description of the employee's day-to-day responsibilities

- A brief description of the individual's past track-record

- A list of the candidate's important achievements

- A list of relevant certifications or special degrees

Each profile should be brief and concise and should take up a paragraph or two. A good profile should include information about the person's educational background, previous employment, relevant skills and any accomplishments, both personal and work-related that may be relevant to your business. You should only include information that is relevant to their role within your business so the reader can easily gain a good idea of how that person will influence the success of your business.

If you are running a sole proprietorship then you should follow this same method but only for yourself. Though it can be easy to talk about yourself and highlight all of your accomplishments, it is important to ensure that you follow the guidelines just as if you were writing about someone else. After you ensure that you've included a profile for your most important members of management, you can then provide brief profiles for any professionals you use to consult your business. For example, if you have an accountant and a lawyer, then you should include a profile for them following your management team.

Selecting an Advisory Board

Small business owners should also consider setting up an advisory board for their business. Having an advisory board shows potential investors that you're serious about making the best business decisions possible. The primary benefit of having an advisory board is that it provides third-party wisdom by means of presentations, discussions and decision-making for your business. Even if you don't have an advisory board ready to describe as you go to write your plan, go ahead and put aside a section to come back to and fill out later. It can be very beneficial for your business in more ways than one.

An advisory board is a group of people who meet on a regular basis to discuss decisions and activities concerning your business. Members of the board are usually appointed or elected for a predetermined number of years. Selecting the members of your advisory board can be a challenging situation. Board members should all possess skills and pieces of knowledge that are reflective of your business but they should also be able to present and utilize new skills and ideas. While advisory board members should generally not be a part of the business itself, some business owners also choose to include their investors on their board.

The best way to find candidates for your advisory board is to figure the areas in which your business needs the most guidance. For example, if one of your company goals is to expand your business from the east coast to the west coast, then you should consider appointing a person with experience in company expansions to your board. Favorable candidates are those who have already been on other advisory boards. Advisory boards are generally small and often consist of 5 to 9 members.

Hiring Non-Management Employees

Finally, you should include a detailed plan on how you plan to hire non-management employees to your team. Your plan should give the reader a clear idea on how many non-managerial employees you will need to run successfully and how much money it will take up in your budget. This is a good section to include payroll/taxation information, if you will be hiring actual employees, or to include copies of contracts and agreements if you will be utilizing independent contractors. You should describe each non-managerial position and note what important skills you will need in each employee as well as include details on compensation, benefits and anything else you will be offering in exchange for employment. Your plan should also include details on recruitment and training.

Chapter 10: Analyze Your Competition

No matter the industry, businesses will always face some kind of competition upon entering the market. Small businesses especially have to take this challenge head on because they can either seize new opportunities before anybody else does or they can quickly fail and shutter for good. Luckily, there are some great strategies that you can utilize to analyze your competition and see what you can do to come out on top. It is also extremely important to include a competition analysis in your plan to show potential investors that you have thoroughly researched your direct competitors to the point where your business has a good chance of staying afloat next to them.

The first strategy is to identify your direct competitors. Your direct competitor is a business in the same industry that is selling the same or similar products as you. For example, an ice cream shop's direct competitors would be the two other ice cream shops in town. An online bookstore's direct competitors would be any other web platforms where you can purchase books. A law firm's direct competitors would be any other law firms, for example.

If you're in an industry with direct competitors both in physical locations and online, you can choose whether to include both at your discretion. For example, if your business is a physical bookstore and there are several online bookstores, it is up to you to decide whether you want to include the online bookstores in your analysis based on different factors such as hours, customer service, etc.

You can find out where and who your direct competitors are by doing a simple Google search, which will usually lay them all out on a map for you. Having a map of where your competition is located is great because you'll also be able to make many educated predictions on how demographics affect their business. You can also look in phone directories or simply drive around town to find your competitors, although I believe that an internet search is the easiest and most thorough way to get a complete list.

Once you have created this list, you can ask yourself some questions in terms of your direct competitors to gain a better idea of where they are in terms of competitive advantage. You can then provide these questions and answers in this section of your plan. The following are some questions to think about:

- What are the strengths of your direct competitor? Their weaknesses?

- Where are they located in comparison to where you will be located? Are there any important differences?

- Who do they target? Is their target audience broad or narrowed down to a specialized group? How does that compare to your target audience?

- What are they really "selling" to their customers? How does that compare or contrast to what you're really "selling?" (Think back to the strategy of selling "speed and ease" instead of "written content" to business coaches)

- What does their marketing plan look like? What marketing platforms and resources do they use? (More on this in the next chapter!)

- Are there any opportunities that they have missed that you can capitalize on?

- What does their growth outlook look like?

- Can you predict what, if anything, they will do when you become their competition?

Instead of asking these questions mentally, it is best to write down each answer so you can include it in this section of your business plan. Having it written down also makes it easier for you and your team to analyze your competitors' strengths and weaknesses. Once you have answered these questions, the key move is to attempt to identify the competitive strategies of your competitors. Once you have identified their strategies, you can then try to identify with the way your competition thinks, which can help you predict their next move, which you can then use to try and capitalize on any important opportunities that they may have missed. Try to analyze your competitors from the customer's point of view; think about things that your customer will take into consideration, such as affordability, customer service, marketing tastes, brand recognition, etc.

SWOT Analysis

Next, you can analyze your business to see where it stands in terms of competitive advantage. The best and most time-tested way to do so is to perform a SWOT Analysis. To begin a SWOT Analysis, you'll want to take is to create a SWOT template. You can do this by hand by drawing a grid with four large squares on a piece of paper or you can create a table in your word processor or easily download a premade template online. Make the top left square **Strengths**, the top right square **Weaknesses,** the lower left square **Opportunities** and the lower right square **Threats.** On the left side of the grid, write **Internal** next to the Strengths and Weaknesses squares and **External** next to the Opportunities and Threats squares. Strengths and weaknesses are based on internal factors of your business but opportunities and threats are influenced by external factors.

In the Strengths square, you will list the strengths of your business that may put it at an advantage over your competitors. In the Weaknesses square, you will list any flaws your business has that may rank it below its direct competitors. Think about factors such as labor, financing, resources and anything else that you can control from within your business when completing these two squares. In the Opportunities square, you will list any business opportunities that you and your team can take advantage of to put the business above its direct competition. In the Threats square, you will brainstorm to list any factors that may threaten your competitive advantage. When working on these two squares, think in terms of factors that you cannot control from within your business – such as technological changes, trends within your target audience, environmental changes, economic changes, etc.

Once all of the squares are filled in, you can then use the information to rewrite everything into cohesive sentences that compare your business to its competition and include this information in this section of your plan.

Performing a SWOT Analysis can provide your readers with a general overview of how your business stands in the sea of competition. The next step is to perform a closer comparison of your products or services to those of your direct competitors. You can compare your products or services in terms of pricing, features, physical build, consumer benefits, materials, etc. You can easily repurpose this information from the section of your plan that focuses on describing your product or service. The most important part of this section, however, is emphasizing its unique value proposition and how it stands next to the competition.

Competitors' Marketing Strategies

Next, it is important to analyze the marketing strategies used by your direct competitors. We will go more into detail on how to develop your own killer marketing plan in the next chapter but for this section, it is most important to first understand the marketing strategy that you'll be working against. Most marketing strategies include blanket marketing, which is basically mass marketing on TV, billboards, magazine ads, etc., digital marketing, which is online marketing through channels such as email, social media websites, websites, etc., outbound marketing such as cold-calling, telemarketing, etc., and inbound marketing such as search-engine optimization utilization.

The most important strategy in completing an analysis of your competitors' marketing strategy is to determine what kind of marketing they're doing and what you can do to gain the competitive advantage. Again, you can simply do this by determining the strengths and weaknesses of their marketing strategy and finding flaws that you can capitalize on. It is especially to look for social trends in designing your own marketing strategy because being on top of the latest trends is a great way to put yourself ahead of the competition.

Finally, you're probably wondering just where and how you will uncover all the information you need on your competitor. It may sound impossible, but the good news is that it's actually pretty easy; you won't even have to play the part of a spy to do it. Usually a quick Google search of your competition will yield more than enough information to work with. Company websites, newspaper articles and other public press sources, LinkedIn profiles, annual industry reports, trade shows and other industry events are great places to look for information.

Chapter 11: Developing Your Marketing Strategy

The last couple of chapters have focused on some very important, but possibly boring, material. However, now it's time for another "fun" section of your plan – your marketing strategy. The primary purpose of a marketing strategy is know how you will market your product or service to your target audience, so that you can make money.

Marketing costs can also easily rack up and become very expensive so it's important to plan how you will budget your money for marketing wisely. It is also important to include the details of your marketing strategy in your business plan so you can demonstrate how your business will both fulfil a need and be highly profitable to potential investors. If you have experience in marketing, you may find it a simple matter to create a great marketing strategy. For the rest of us, however, the learning curve begins here. Many businesses outsource, hiring marketing experts to work with them on developing a marketing plan for their products and services.

Let's begin this chapter with a brief overview of marketing and some of the best marketing strategies. Marketing is the method of promoting your product or service to your target audience. There are many different ways that a business can market its products or service. Some traditional and time-tested methods of marketing include billboards, television ads, newspaper ads, snail mail ads, magazine ads and telemarketing to name a few.

Every channel of marketing is often somehow related to the product or service. For example, a magazine ad for a new men's cologne would be more likely to appear in a men's magazine rather than in a magazine targeted to women. With all of the development in technology over the last decade, there is also many ways to market to a target audience through digital methods.

Digital marketing methods include email marketing, web banners, social media marketing and most importantly, search engine optimization. Search engine optimization helps websites rank high in search engines through the use of keywords that potential customers may be typing into the search bar.

Since there are tons of ways to market your product or service to your target audience, as well as tons of strategies to really leave a lasting impact on them, it is important to create a marketing strategy plan to present as part of your business plan.

Creating a Marketing Strategy Plan

Your marketing strategy plan is where you put together everything you know about marketing, effectively portraying your killer marketing strategy that is intended to help your business become extremely profitable.

Beginning to create your marketing strategy plan is easy. You may be surprised to see that your marketing plan will mostly consist of information you've already gathered and included in the section of your plan where you created your industry and marketing analysis. I know that some people experience negative emotions and second-guess themselves when they repeat information, which happens a lot in business plans, so if you are one of those people then you can simply pretend you are writing your marketing strategy plan separately from your business plan.

Your marketing plan should include four main sections:

1. Describing Your Market – You will already have this information on hand after completing your industry outlook in Chapter 7. As the first section of your marketing plan, you will simply need to restate the information you gathered regarding your market and the industry within which you will be doing business

2. Describing Your Ideal Client – You will have already created an ideal client profile. It can simply be copied into

this section. Include every detail, no matter how seemingly insignificant.

3. Competition Marketing Analysis – Think back to the previous chapter, where you analyzed all aspects of your competition. If at that time you didn't perform a deep analysis of the competition's marketing strategies, now is the time to do so. A clear understanding of your competitors' marketing strategies can help you identify areas where your business can shine. Look for gaps in their marketing and position yourself to take advantage of these opportunities.

4. Your Marketing Strategy – This section will be the longest and will probably require the most work. It should include information on your overall marketing strategy, including your marketing budget, your branding strategies and pricing strategies. You should include mention of your marketing distribution channels and the marketing platforms you plan to utilize.

Developing a Marketing Budget

One of the first and most important parts of your marketing strategy is your marketing budget. As I mentioned at the beginning of this chapter, marketing can quickly become highly expensive. It is important to clearly state how much money is available for marketing and to demonstrate that you're spending it wisely.

Fortunately, it's easy to create a marketing budget, even if you've never done this before. According to the Small Business Association, a good rule of thumb is to set aside 7% of your revenue for marketing if your annual revenue is less than five million dollars. However, there are a few things to consider when it comes to managing your budget:

Define Tools And Resources

You'll need to predict the kinds of marketing tools and resources you will want to utilize for your business. Some business owners prefer to host a high quality website with plenty of videos and animation. Others prefer a dominant social media presence, using tracking tools to keep their finger on the pulse of the market, frequently analyzing where their customers are coming from.

Resources such as websites, marketing tools, and market research applications all come with a price tag attached, so it's important to define what you're going to need early on. You'll need to come up with a rough estimate of how much money you'll need to support these tools and resources.

Advertising Fees

Next, you'll want to estimate your advertising costs. Advertising is a form of marketing that attempts to gather new prospective customers through boosting awareness. If you've ever heard a commercial on the radio or have seen a billboard while driving down the highway, you are a recipient of advertising. Common forms of advertisement include "ads" in channels such as newspapers, magazines, radio, and television. Ads can also consist of online banners and online or in-person events, such as hosting a table at a local festival.

Track Your Results

Finally, it is essential to monitor what your money is doing for you. Consider it a return on investment If you notice that one type of marketing is working better than another, it would make sense to invest more money there, and less on the method that isn't working as effectively.

The entire purpose of marketing is to help your business generate more customers and ultimately bring in more money. You definitely want to know where you're getting the most "bang for your buck" in terms of marketing.

Developing a Pricing Strategy

Pricing your products and services is another huge factor that can affect your marketing effectiveness. There is a science to consumer psychology; pricing is closely related to both perception of quality and the attractiveness of an item. Consequently, it's very important to work out the best pricing strategy for your specific products and services.

I've included some of the most effective strategies here. You can mix and match these strategies, experimenting and finding what works best for your specific situation:

- Economy Pricing – This pricing strategy promotes products and services at the lowest price possible while emphasizing great value. Many companies such as Budget Airlines or Walmart's grocery section utilize this pricing strategy.

- Penetration Pricing – This pricing strategy attracts new customers with low to free pricing at first. They then gradually raise their rates.

- Premium Pricing – This pricing strategy enables your business to charge higher prices than your direct competitors, because your consumers are purchasing a something of unique value. Consumers are usually willing to pay higher prices for something they believe is of premium quality.

- Bundling – With this pricing strategy, a business sells a combined group of products or services for one price, thus passing greater value onto the consumer. It's also a common way for businesses to get rid of "leftover" stock or to boost awareness of lesser-known items.

- Upselling – This pricing strategy enables a business to charge a second fee by offering their consumers something extra after they have locked in to buying a basic product or service. If a fast food worker has ever offered you a larger sized drink for only 50 cents more or if a movie theater offered reserved seats for only $3 extra, that would be an example of upselling.

- Complementary Pricing – This pricing strategy enables a business to sell a core product at a low price with more expensive extras that the consumer will need to buy in order to continue using the product or service. For example, many phone companies sell preloaded cell phones at lower prices than major phone companies, but the customer will be required to purchase additional minutes of service in order to continue using the phone.

- Promotional Pricing – This pricing strategy is common and is mainly used to attract new customers. It can often help businesses move old product out the door. You may have walked into a grocery store and seen a sign that said all bakery items are "buy one, get one free" because they're expiring soon. You may have also received a coupon in the mail from a dentist offering a "new patient special" at a highly discounted rate. These are all examples of promotional pricing

Other factors you may want to consider in your pricing strategy are the demand curve for your product or service, your fixed and variable costs, profit maximization, and environmental factors or regulations (for example, many states have a minimum price at which cigarettes may be sold).

Selecting Your Distribution Channels

Your distribution channel strategy explains to the reader how you will get your product or service to your customers. Having a distribution plan in place is important because different methods of distribution can have varying factors such as cost. Some distribution channels are simple and some can be a bit more complicated so it is important to ensure that all information related to your distribution strategy is clear and aligns well with your overall marketing strategy. Selecting your distribution channel is also important for building a consistent reputation with your customers. Customers who find it easy to obtain your products or services are more likely to continue doing business with you.

The most common types of distribution channels are direct sales, wholesaling, mail-ordering, and online sales. Direct selling is efficient but it is also very hands-on, which can distract you from your focus on producing a quality product or service.

Wholesaling is beneficial for businesses whose customers are disperse but the main drawback is that you may lose out on a portion of the final sale price. Mail-ordering is probably the least expensive distribution method; however, you must have a very specific target audience for it to be effective.

Online sales are probably the best and most popular method of distribution and it is easily accessible by customers from anywhere in the world. It is also getting easier and easier to align your marketing strategy with online sales, increasing the chances that your customers will buy.

In determining which distribution channels are best for your business, you may need to perform additional market research (yes, *more* research!) about your target audience. You will need to figure out their buying preferences and will subsequently need to determine how you can complement their buying preferences with your own marketing strategies. For example, many readers have begun to rely on purchasing books from major online outlets, such as Amazon, instead of purchasing them from a physical book store.

Authors who choose to publish books through a publishing platform called CreateSpace have the option to select the Amazon storefront as one of their distribution channels to help boost their sales. Part of the author's marketing strategy then may be to utilize Amazon's free or discounted ebook promotions to further help push recently published books to the forefront.

Chapter 12: Revenue, Expenses, and Financial Planning

This section of your business plan is the most important. It will explain to the reader how all of the numbers back up everything that you have planned. Financial planning is the key to launching a successful business; when the numbers don't work out, the business is likely to fail.

Before you fill out your financial plan, your business plan is just an idea. As you begin to fill in the numbers, it starts to become real before your eyes. Naturally, a solid financial plan will also assure potential investors not only that your business has a great chance of success, but also that you have a grasp on how to work your money effectively. In this section, you will discover how to write a well-based financial plan that will serve as the foundation for your business. You will likely discover in the process that spreadsheets are your best friend; they really can help you manage the financials associated with your business!

A basic financial plan should include a **profit and loss statement, a balance sheet,** and **a cash flow sheet**. The purpose of these resources is to show where your business currently stands and to assist you in setting realistic financial forecasts and making financial decisions.

Profit-Loss Statement

A profit and loss statement is a snapshot of the money coming in, the money coming out, and tracks much money you spent on expenses within a specific quarter. In a nutshell, it will tell you what your net profit is by subtracting your revenue from your expenses. Profit and loss statements are good over the long term to show you how your business is progressing from quarter to quarter. It can also spot potential problems so you can deal with them before they endanger your solvency.

To create a profit and loss statement, you begin by listing the name of your business at the top of the document, followed by the title (profit and loss statement), followed by the date range included in the report. Your report will usually be generated on a quarterly basis, so it will reflect the totals for three months of business.

Below the header you will list – in separate sections, first how much, in dollars, you sold, then your expenses for that time period. At the bottom you subtract the expenses from your sales, to get your gross profit.

everything included in your operating revenue followed by a total. It should then list your total amount of expenses, followed by your gross profit, which is your total operating revenue minus your total amount of expenses. It should then list everything included in your overhead, followed by an overhead total, which should then be deducted from your gross profit. This is known as your operating income. You should then list any other expenses and deduct them from your operating income. Finally, you should deduct the total amount of income tax you will need to pay on your revenue from your operating income. The final number is your **net profit,** which should be the last figure in your profit and loss statement.

Balance Sheet

A balance sheet is a statement that provides an overview of your assets, liabilities and equity of your shareholders. A good way to view a balance sheet is to see it as an equation where your assets are your equities minus your liabilities. A business must balance out money that it borrows and money it receives from its investors to be able to exist and generate money. Your assets include, cash revenue, physical inventory, and accounts on which customers have pending payments. Liabilities would be debt, interest, rent, taxes, and payable wages.

To create a balance sheet, prepare a document with the name of your business at the top, followed by the title (balance sheet), and by its creation date. You will then list all of your company's assets on the right side of the document, broken down by category, with a grand total at the end. On the left side of the page, you will do the same with your liabilities and equities. The key is to ensure that your total assets match the total amount of your liabilities and equities.

Cash Flow

A cash flow sheet is a statement that provides an overview of how much cash and cashable assets are flowing through your business. The main difference between a cash flow sheet and a profit and loss statement is that it doesn't show pending payments. It won't show accounts receivable, where payments have not yet been processed and deposited in the business account. Instead, your cash flow is measured within your operations, investments, and in anything that you finance.

To create a cash flow sheet, at the top of your document you will write the name of your business, the title of the report (cash flow sheet) and the timeframe for which the statement reports. Next, you will create three different columns. This is where you will list the individual components of the cash flow from your operations, investments, and anything you finance. At the bottom of the document, you will sum up your total amount of cash flow.

New businesses may not have some of the information required to create the three documents listed above. Instead, they will include a sales forecast in the financial section of their plan. A sales forecast is generally a three to five year outlook on what the business believes they can achieve in terms of revenue. The most important piece of advice in creating your financial plan is to do so with practicality in mind. Outrageous or unrealistic numbers will not lead your way to success and it's likely that a potential investor will question numbers that don't make sense. Whether you're just including a sales forecast or if you're including hypothesized profit and loss, cash flow and balance sheets, realistic numbers are definitely the more important way to go.

Tracking Expenses

Many new businesses may also find it helpful to include a breakdown of expenses. Some businesses may have few to no expenses, but others may have so many expenses it will be necessary to list them out. Either way, listing your expenses is helpful in creating your expense budget.

Your expense list should include expenses that are fixed, such as rent or insurance, and expenses that are variable, such as the cost of resources. New businesses should also include a list of expenses that are exclusive to initial start-up costs, such as the cost of registering the business with the state.

Again, even if your expenses are initial estimates, it still enables you to come up with a ballpark range of how much money you'll need to put toward expenses. It is important to remember that even if you predict your sales or the amount of your expenses, you can always go back and edit your forecasts to include the actual numbers. This then enables you to look for patterns and trends to make your future predictions even more accurate.

It is important to revisit your financial plan at least once a year to ensure that your numbers accurately reflect where your business stands in the present time.

Chapter 13: Funding Strategies

Last but not least is the final piece you'll need to get your business off the ground – how to get funding. Rarely, a few first-time business owners are able to completely fund the launching of their first business all by themselves. However, in the majority of cases, you'll need to find some financial backing. That's what this chapter is all about. By the time you're finished, you should have a handle on what you need to do to secure the financial foundation to start your business.

Investors

Funding isn't the only reason to attract a team of investors. Besides money, investors often offer you wise counsel based on decades of their own experiences. Sometimes investors will stay behind the scenes, but other times they are willing to play a more participative role in your business. The great news is that you aren't limited to your friends and family. You can easily attract third-party investors, as long as you can clearly portray what they will get in exchange for funding your business. To this end, your business plan will be the strongest tool on your belt.

There are two basic types of investors: **venture capitalists** and **angel investors**. Venture capitalists are more willing to sink money into startup businesses with entrepreneurs who have little to no experience, in hopes that they will receive back a major return on their investment.

An angel investor, on the other hand, is a wealthy individual who provides financial backing to a company in exchange for a percentage of ownership in the business. Angel investors are more likely to be family members or close friends of the business owner. Their trust tends to be based more on you as a person than on the viability of the business. Aside from people you may already know, you can often find potential investors at business networking events. It is always best to personally meet with your investors rather than presenting your idea over the phone or via the internet.

What To Look For In An Investor

Many first-time business owners assume that *anyone* who is willing to financially back their business is a worthy investor, but it is critical that you choose your investors wisely. This requires some personal responsibility as well as knowing what to look for in a great investor.

As a business owner, it is important that you practice excellent communication skills. If you're the type of business owner who cannot even be bothered to pick up your phone when it rings or respond to an email in a prompt manner, then it is going to be very difficult to secure investors. Your investors will want to be confident that you will correspond with them as efficiently as possible, especially since their money is involved in the endeavor.

You will also want to present yourself as an honest and moral business owner. If you are not up front with your investors about how their money is going to play out in your business, then you'll have a hard time finding anyone who wants to do business with you.

Equally important, you must consistently display your utmost confidence in your business. Nobody is going to want to put money into your business if *you* can't even sound confident about its chances of success! When presenting your business to potential investors, the trick is to pretend that your business is fully funded and successful, no matter what things look like at the moment. This is more likely to help you sound confident and it also counts as a powerful visualization technique.

Put Your Money Where Your Mouth Is

Another great trick is to invest some of your own capital in your business before you begin looking for a team of investors. Once others see that you've already put your own money into your company, it shows that you are convinced the business will be successful, making it more likely for them to be convinced of its potential success.

Of course, your investors should also mirror the same traits they are looking for in you. You'll want to be confident you're dealing with people who can correspond efficiently and also be open and honest. In this respect you are also evaluating them; their investment is a form of partnership.

There are several additional qualities to look for in your quest for potential investors. First, you'll want a team of investors who are committed and persistent. Optimism goes a very long way too, especially in the business world where there are always contingencies you haven't dreamed of. When the unthinkable happens, you'll want to know you're working with a group of people who will refuse to give up and back out without exploring every possible option for success.

You'll also want to choose investors who are rich in experience and who can bring varied ideas to the table. Having a team of investors who all think alike can get decisions made quickly, but your team will be ultimately much more powerful when each member has something unique to offer the group as a whole is committed to hearing each member.

There are several important factors that potential investors will look for before they can be convinced to back you. While investors tend to prefer backing experienced entrepreneurs, you can minimize the impact of your limitations by presenting a business plan that is strong, solid, and convincing. Your presentation should focus most of its attention on finances, the sections that describe your products and services, the description of your target audience and the plans for your management team. Investors are also more likely to back your business if you can present an idea that has the potential to be truly revolutionary or life-changing.

Once you've selected your investors, it is important to write up a contract that spells out the terms and conditions between you, your business, and your investors. Setting out the rules before everybody gets involved is essential to prevent future conflicts. Negotiating a contract between you and your investors shows that you are truly serious about the success of your business and provides another evidence that you are well worth their investment.

Other Funding Options

Bank Loans

Aside from investors, a business loan from a bank is the next most obvious funding option. Presenting your completed business plan to the loan officer at your bank is every bit as important as presenting it to potential investors. At the same time, there are some key differences between a bank loan and money from investors.

The first difference is that any money the bank lends you is entirely yours to oversee. While investors may expect you to account for how you use their money, not so with a bank; all they care about is that they receive their regular repayments.

The second major difference is that unlike investors, banks do not require any ownership in your business. Another benefit of utilizing a bank loan is that they often come with low interest rates and high credit limits. Some disadvantages of utilizing a bank loan are the lengthy application process, coupled with banks' hesitancy to give out loans to new small businesses.

Grants

Many small businesses find that grant money is a great funding strategy. Grants are usually offered by government agencies, nonprofits, and other philanthropic foundations. One unique factor about grants is that they each have specific demographics they are targeting for their gifts. For example, many grants are specifically targeted to women. One is a grant is for Asian women in business who live and work in low-income areas of Washington, D.C., so you can see the level of detail you'll need to watch for when you're doing your research.

Grant applications are a whole 'nother proposition entirely. Each grant will specify the information that must be included in the application, often dictating its structure, and you must follow these instructions to a "T." While you can't just mail in your business plan (although sometimes that may be a welcomed attachment), the process of generating it has equipped you with pretty much any information a foundation will ask of you.

Grants are often worth the little extra effort that goes into preparing the application. Government agencies sometimes offer grants in hopes of stimulating local economies by creating jobs, and in the process, generating more taxes. A simple Internet search can help you narrow down the field and choose grants that are most likely to respond favorably to your business.

Crowdfunding

Crowdfunding is a relatively recent strategy entrepreneurs are using to fund their ventures. If you are familiar with websites such as Kickstarter, then you already have an idea of what crowdfunding is about. It is basically a system where individuals contribute money to a business or product that they believe would be cool or useful.

Kickstarter, for example, allows "backers" to select an amount of money they want to invest into the business or idea. Business owners can incentivize the backers by offering a small reward in exchange for their investment. For example, a person investing $10 into a video project may get his or her name in the credits, while a person investing $100 into the project may get a chance to be in the video. While it can truly help get innovative products to market, crowdfunding is also highly competitive, so you need to be very careful when you use it. Because the concept is so popular, many ideas fail to earn the funds they need to become a reality.

401k

Although this method isn't a used frequently to supply emergency funding, you can always dip into your 401k for support, as long as you pay the money back within a certain timeframe, usually a year.

Credit Cards

When all else fails, your final option is to open up a personal credit card to fund your business. However, you should only use this as a last resort, since interest rates on personal credit cards tend to be very high.

Conclusion

I hope this book has helped you craft a powerful business plan that will amaze potential investors, get your business off to a successful start and benefit the people in your target audience.

Your next step is to turn your dream business into a successful reality. Review the entire book, fleshing out the parts of your business plan that need additional work. Do the necessary research and write up the results that support your venture. Solicit feedback and advice from small business organizations and successful entrepreneurs. To develop the document itself, download a premade template online or simply create your own, using the guidelines in the previous chapters. I would also highly recommend OneNote or EverNote for keeping track of your business. They are incredible!

After you've completed the first draft of your business plan (remember, this document will grow and evolve along with your business, so it's never really finalized), your next step is to choose your business funding strategy. Once you've obtained the right amount of funding, you're ready to turn your plan into reality. It's time to get out there and start living your dream as a successful entrepreneur.

I wish you the best of luck! May your entrepreneurial endeavors succeed beyond your wildest dreams! I'd love to hear of your success.

Thanks for reading.

If this book helped you or someone you know in any way, then please spare a few moments right now to leave a nice review.

My Other Books

Be sure to check out my author page to learn more about me and see my other books at:

USA:
https://www.amazon.com/author/susanhollister

UK: http://amzn.to/2qiEzA9

Or simply type my name in the search bar: Susan Hollister

Thank You

Made in the USA
San Bernardino, CA
25 January 2019